A
LONDON CHILD
OF THE
1870s

A
LONDON CHILD
OF THE
1870s

M. V. HUGHES

OXFORD NEW YORK TORONTO MELBOURNE
OXFORD UNIVERSITY PRESS

Oxford University Press, Walton Street, Oxford OX2 6DP

OXFORD   LONDON   GLASGOW   NEW YORK   TORONTO
MELBOURNE   WELLINGTON   CAPE TOWN   NAIROBI
DAR ES SALAAM   KUALA LUMPUR   SINGAPORE   JAKARTA
HONG KONG   TOKYO   DELHI   BOMBAY   CALCUTTA
MADRAS   KARACHI

First published as *A London Child of the Seventies*, 1934
Re-issued as Part I of the trilogy *A London Family 1870–1900*, 1946.
First issued as an Oxford Paperback 1977
Reprinted 1978, 1979, 1980

British Library Cataloguing Publication Data

Hughes, Mary Vivian
   A London Child of the 1870s.
   ISBN 0-19-281216-5
   1. Title
   942.1'081'0924   DA688
   London–Social life and customs

*Reproduced, printed and bound in Great Britain by
Cox & Wyman Ltd., Reading*

CONTENTS

	Preface	1
I.	*'A Star Danced'*	3
II.	*Ups and Downs*	13
III.	*Round the Year*	21
IV.	*Sailing near the Wind*	30
V.	*Up to Eleven*	41
VI.	*School-days*	54
VII.	*Sunday*	67
VIII.	*Callers*	77
IX.	*A Long Railway Journey*	85
X.	*Reskadinnick*	92
XI.	*Outdoor Doings*	102
XII.	*Indoor Doings*	118
XIII.	*A Family Club*	125
XIV.	*A Last Christmas*	135

PREFACE

NONE of the characters in this book are fictitious. The incidents, if not dramatic, are at least genuine memories. *Expressions of jollity and enjoyment of life are understatements rather than overstatements. We were just an ordinary, suburban, Victorian family, undistinguished ourselves and unacquainted with distinguished people. It occurred to me to record our doings only because, on looking back, and comparing our lot with that of the children of to-day, we seemed to have been so* lucky. *In writing them down, however, I have come to realize that luck is at one's own disposal, that 'there is nothing either good or bad but thinking makes it so'. Bring up children in the conviction that they are lucky, and behold they are. But in our case high spirits were perhaps inherited, as my story will show.*

DON PEDRO. *In faith, lady, you have a merry heart.*
BEATRICE. *Yea, my lord; I thank it, poor fool, it keeps on the windy side of care.*

'A Star Danced'

A GIRL with four brothers older than herself is born under a lucky star. To be brought up in London, in the eighteen-seventies, by parents who knew how to laugh at both jokes and disasters, was to be under the influence of Jupiter himself.

This fell to my lot. My early memories run from 1870, when we moved into a big house in Canonbury, until 1879, when my happy childhood was abruptly ended. I hope to show that Victorian children did not have such a dull time as is usually supposed.

It is true that we had few toys, few magazines, few outside entertainments, and few means of getting about. But we got so much out of the few we had, by anticipation, by 'saving up', by exhaustive observation of the shop windows, and by the utmost use of the things we did achieve, that the well-to-do child of to-day can never get the same kind of pleasure. The modern ready-made well-stocked farm-yard, stable, or railway station, after a few days' admiration, asks for nothing but destruction, for there is nothing else to do about it.

For us, a large box of plain bricks was the foundation of all our doings. It served for railway stations, docks, forts, towers, and every kind of house. Another box of bricks, thin and flat with dove-tailed edges, enabled us to build long walls around our cities. Some two dozen soldiers, red for English and blue for French, mostly wounded and disarmed, carried out grand manœuvres on specimens of granite and quartz arranged on the mantelpiece, and were easily mobilized anywhere. A packing-case did for a shop, where goods of all kinds were sold for marbles or shells or foreign stamps. The whole room was occasionally the sea, where a chair turned upside down was the *Great Eastern*, well and truly launched on the floor, for laying the Atlantic cable. A fat Lemprière's *Dictionary* did for a quay or a transport wagon or an enemy town.

We had several remains of ninepins, and plenty of marbles. I loved the colours of the marbles and furtively collected them. Their relative merits I knew, and how to prize a 'blood alley'; but learn to play I never could, preferring to flick or throw the marble, instead of using the thumb in the masterly way that the boys insisted on.

A new toy was an event. Each one of our well-worn treasures must have made a sensation when it first arrived. One such event is graven on my memory. It was my fifth birthday, and I got up early and ran into my parents' room to be greeted. Laid out on the floor was a large and resplendent horse and cart. The horse was dapple-grey, all prancing and eyeing me in a friendly, willing way. The bright yellow cart, whose new stickiness I can still feel, had a movable back-piece that you could do something with. It would 'take off', and if you moved a wooden pin the cart tipped up; then you said 'gee-up' to the horse and all the goods would fall out. I had seen it done in the street, and promised myself no end of pleasure carting bricks for the boys.

Whether by design or not, we were allowed almost unlimited freedom, to imperil our lives without any sense of fear, and to invent our own amusements. We never had a nurse, or a nursery, or any one to supervise us. Instead of this we were given a room to ourselves—*all* to ourselves. In this matter we were better off than any other children we knew then or have known since. For our parents did the thing thoroughly. They provided a large table, a warm carpet, a fire whenever we liked, a large ottoman for storage and to serve as a window-seat; and left everything else to us. We chose the wall-paper and put what pictures we liked on the walls.

This room, which became a happy memory for us all through our lives, was called the 'study'—perhaps as a hint of its intention. The name added to its dignity without putting, as far as we were concerned, any notion of work into it. As time went on we did our home lessons in it, but the word 'study' is always associated in my mind with sheer fun.

So greatly was our possession of the study respected that I cannot remember my father or mother ever being in it, except on the occasions when they sat in the stalls during one of our theatrical displays, paying heavily for the privilege and for the programmes.

In one recess of the study there were four shelves, and by common consent each boy had one to himself. On his shelf he displayed his treasures. I remember the awe with which I gazed at my second brother's box of mathematical instruments, with bright compasses fitted into blue velvet grooves, and an ivory ruler that shifted into two for some strange purpose. He also had a big magnifying glass, which I always imagined had to be used when one 'magnified the Lord' in church. Some geological specimens were also displayed, but seemed to me of no use except for building forts.

My third brother, Charles, had quite other tastes. He was all for colour and variety, and one never knew what he would do next. At one time he had a rage for churches, and used to visit all the places of worship in the neighbourhood to see what they did. Then he arranged a cross and candles and flowers on his shelf, and got bits of coloured silk from mother to make the correct liturgical changes, and I thus early learnt to expect purple in Lent, green for Trinity, and so on, and was able to impress many an elder who had 'really never noticed'.

However, the main attraction for us all was the window. Our house stood at the corner of two roads, and our window had a good view down most of the length of one of them— Grange Road, affording us plenty of information of the doings of our neighbours and any passers-by. Up and down there went, much oftener than to-day, the hawkers of various goods, each with an appropriate cry: 'Flowers all a-blowing and a-growing', 'Ornaments for your fire-stove' (unbelievably hideous streamers of coloured paper), 'A pair of fine soles', bird-cages, iron-holders, brooms, brushes, and baskets. The long, wailing cry was a signal for us to crowd on to the ottoman to watch. Seeing our faces, the hawker would stop, look up eagerly, and hold up his goods. Several times we sent one round to the back-door with the encouraging words 'Mamma would like some.' Then we went to the top of the stairs to listen to the drama below: the hawker telling the housemaid that the Missus said she wanted a bird-cage, pause for journey of inquiry to the Missus, indignant denials, the return, abusive language from the hawker, a slammed door, glee in the study.

My second brother, who liked to talk about 'science', brought out the idea one day that a stone, if you wrapped it in a cloth, wouldn't break glass. We dared him to try it on the window. He said, oh yes, but perhaps it would be better to make it go some distance. We then suggested his trying it on the next-door-but-one's conservatory. I ran down to fetch a stone from the garden, and this was duly tied up in his hand-kerchief. He had been dared, and from a 'dare' there was no retreat. Whizz it went—crash through the glass roof. At this with one accord we became absorbed in pursuits of a studious nature, and after a bit began to feel that the affair had blown over. But then came a message by the housemaid that Master Vivian was wanted in the dining-room. There sat a frail old lady with mother, who was holding the stone-laden handker-chief, marked with Vivian's full name. Mother was breathing out the direst punishments on him, but the injured one was pleading that she only wanted it not to happen again, and it didn't matter at all, that boys would be boys, bless them, she only wished she had a child of her own, and so on, until poor old Vivian was a mush of contrition.

In one of our amusements we were far ahead of the children of the time. My mother had a hobby, amounting to a passion, for water-colour painting, and she encouraged us in every way to draw and paint. She herself had a very large box of colours, and she gave me a little one made of wood, and a bigger, black-metal one to Charles, who could soon draw and paint far better than she could. She besought us at frequent intervals not to suck the brush. But you could never get a good point without sucking a bit, and since mother laid so much stress on the evil effects of green (instant death apparently in some cases), we came to think that the other colours were not so bad.

We were rich too in another way, richer, so far as I can observe, than the average children of to-day. Our parents had accumulated a large number of books, which we were allowed to browse in as much as we liked. Scott, Dickens, Thackeray, Lamb, George Eliot, Tennyson, Byron, Coleridge, Disraeli, these were not 'taught' at school, or set as holiday tasks, but became part of our lives. The elder ones discussed them at table, and quoted from them, till the Micawbers and Becky Sharp and Lamb appeared to my childish mind as some former friends of mother's, whom I recognized with delight later on when I read the books for myself. Rawdon was my eldest brother's favourite, and I knew 'same which I shot Captain Marker' long before I had the faintest notion of its meaning.

Occasionally the discussions became acrimonious. My eldest brother was one day making disparaging remarks about Tennyson, and my mother, all agitated in defence of her idol, fetched his poems from the shelf, and with a 'Listen now, children' began to declaim *Locksley Hall*. When she reached 'I to herd with narrow foreheads' she burst out, flinging down the book, 'What awful rubbish this is!'

That was one of the jolly points about mother—she never minded saying what a fool she had been, was always proud to learn anything from the boys, and never gave us the 'Grown-up people know best' reproof.

I suppose there was a fear on my mother's part that I should be spoilt, for I was two years younger than the youngest boy. To prevent this danger she proclaimed the rule 'Boys first'. I came last in all distribution of food at table, treats of sweets, and so on. I was expected to wait on the boys, run messages, fetch things left upstairs, and never grumble, let alone refuse. All this I thoroughly enjoyed, because I loved running about, and would often dash up and down stairs just to let off my spirits. Of course mother came in for some severe criticism from relations in this matter, but I have never ceased to thank her for this bit of early training.

The boys never failed to smile their thanks, call me 'good girl', do anything for me that wanted a strong thumb or a long arm, and to bring me home something when they had been out and I was left at home. At one time, for instance, I collected threepenny bits, and Charles walked home one day rather than spend this, his last coin, on a tram, so that he might bring it to me.

I have never been able to decide which brother I liked best, for each had some special attraction for me. All four were absurdly unlike in character and appearance, and yet so close in age and size that no stranger could pick out the eldest.

First came Tom. His name was not the short for anything, although his school authorities, in inscribing a prize, tried to dignify it in Latin by rendering the dative 'Tomato', providing us with a nickname for him at once. Tom always took my part through thick and thin, and would take me into partnership when I lost heavily at vingt-et-un. He told me that he had kissed my head when I was only one night old. I found it hard to believe that I had ever been so young. 'You couldn't walk or talk then,' he would say, 'you couldn't even sit up.' 'Oh, Tom,' I would protest, 'I *could* sit *up*!'

He used to take me on his knee and sing nursery rhymes or scraps from music-hall songs, jerking me up and down all the time. This he called doing the 'Jackley Troop', and I would clamour for it again and again.

My second brother had mother's family name of Vivian. This I could not pronounce in my early days, and turned it into Dymond, which soon became Dym. He was the only one who took kindly to school-work, and devoted himself to mathematics. Reserved almost to being morose at times, he was a bit lonely, and was glad to have me as a confidante. He had a secret love of poetry, and would get me up into the study alone and read aloud to me. He had a marvellously modulated voice, now tender, now thunderous. As I sat on the floor in open-mouthed admiration, he let himself go, moving me to pity over Sir Federigo's falcon, and to great excitement over the poor jester who cried out, 'I am, I *am* the King!'

Sometimes, too, he would show me a real scientific experiment. One day he said, 'Molly, would you like to see me turn water into wine, like it is in the Bible?' And he held up two wine-glasses full of water. 'Now watch,' he said, as he poured both into a bigger glass. And actually as I looked the water turned into claret. After this I was ready to believe almost anything. But one day he tried my credulity too hard. With quite a straight face he told me that the Earth was always moving. If it had been one of the other boys, I should have enjoyed the joke, and turned it off with an easy laugh, for they were always taking me in over something. But I didn't expect this from Dym, and his absurdity annoyed me. I can see myself now, in a starched pink frock sticking out all round, and a fat little bare leg with a white sock and shiny black shoe, stamping firmly on the floor and insisting, 'It doesn't, it doesn't!'—as solid in my own conviction as ever Galileo was in his. *Eppur non si muove* was *my* mental reservation.

My third brother, Charles, was the only clever one among us. He worked hard at music and painting, but at nothing else would he do a stroke that could be avoided. He was clever enough to make the tiniest bit of information do the work of volumes. He would find some remote fact about Zenobia or Savonarola, or some one like that, and then pretend to be shocked at the ignorance of those around him. Of course the family knew him, but his trick carried him far with outsiders. He was known to boast that he had never failed in an examination, while the family knew that he had never been in for one. In our continual arguments Charles always seemed to come out top, and his criticisms were merciless. As for me, I was snubbed continually, especially if I fished for a compliment or showed any symptom of self-pity. If I appeared in a new hat (very rare) Charles would exclaim, 'Well! of all the . . .' He often told me how plain I was, and prophesied that I would grow fat like Aunt Polly. But there was rich compensation for all this in the things he would draw for me, the tunes he would play for me to dance, and the long exotic stories he would tell me, in the style of the Arabian Nights, making them up as he went along. And he was kind in unexpected ways, and when people weren't looking.

Nearest in age to me came Barnholt, and nearest in ideas and pleasant childishness. He had a sneaking interest in my dolls and foolish fancies. Lessons of all kinds were a never-ending burden to him. While Tom was good at Latin, Dym at mathematics, and Charles at music and drawing, poor old Barnholt shone in no direction. He would get me to hear him his 'po'try' and what he called 'me drivtivs'—lists of words to be learnt by heart, all derived from some Latin root. The only poem I can recall is Wordsworth's 'Pet Lamb'. What anguish it cost him to get it right! I don't think he ever got beyond the first verse. What insane master could set such a poem to healthy boys? The others used to tease him about it at meal-times, with invitations to 'Drink, pretty creature, drink'. Chaff, of course, Barnholt enjoyed, as one of the alleviations of home life, but detentions at school—they were the curse.

While anything smelling of school-work was poison to Barnholt, any little job of practical work, any errand, any risky adventure proposed, and he was on the spot. 'I say, Barney, do rope this box for me.' 'You might run and fetch me some stamps.' 'Look here, Barney, *you* go first.' There was no record of a refusal.

For some reason, different in each case perhaps, Barnholt was every one's favourite. In a moment of confidence Dym told me how, long ago, the family had gone for a holiday, leaving Barnholt, a tiny boy, with the servants (for some un-known reason). 'We came back unexpectedly', said Dym, 'and I ran ahead and caught sight of Barney in the window.' Here Dym shuddered as he added, 'His face was such a picture of misery that I have never been able to forget it.'

One reason, common to us all, for loving Barnholt a bit extra came from an incident of his fifth year. Although it happened when I was too young to know anything about it, I heard the story often enough to make the details always clear to me, even to the name of the culprit. This was a girl,

Emma Lazelle, who took the four boys out for a walk one afternoon. I should have been taken too, no doubt, only that perambulators were newfangled things in those days, and we never had one; a baby too big to be carried stayed at home. In due course the party returned to tea, and only then discovered that Barnholt was missing.

'Where did you see him last?' 'Who was he walking with?' 'Where did you go?' 'Why didn't you keep looking round?' Mother rained such questions on Emma's head, without waiting for replies. But when she caught the word 'canal', and realized that Barnholt might have fallen into it, she stopped talking and faced despair. Fortunately my father came home soon, and went at once to the Police Station, assuring mother that the canal was out of the question. He did not elaborate his reasons for this statement, but it acted well. He drew blank at the Police Station, but was told that inquiries would be made.

Mother belonged to that school of thought that hopes to hasten a person's return by watching the road. For three nights and the best part of three days she hardly left the dining-room window which commanded the front gate. Strange to say, even the neighbours whose names we didn't know were interested. The wives saw mother hour after hour in the window, and the husbands talked it over with my father in the train going to the City. It was this kind of primitive S.O.S. that was successful at last, for the police in those days had no efficient means of rapid communication.

On the afternoon of the third day, when mother had begun to lose heart and strength, the gate was pushed open, and a neighbour from the house opposite ran up our path waving her hand excitedly. Mother rushed to the door and heard the words blurted out, 'Your little boy is found.' The watch at the window was now a different business, and presently a policeman appeared leading Barnholt by the hand. The little fellow looked very jolly, and his first words were never forgotten: 'Are those for me?'—as he spied some ripe gooseberries on the table.

It seemed that he had wandered far afield, had been found by a policeman, and could give no information beyond that his name was Barney, his mother's was Mamma, and he lived in the 'black house'. (This was because the next door to us had been newly painted, making ours look dirty.) The police had evidently been kind to him, but all that he was ever able to tell us was that they had given him some bread and butter and a halfpenny. In fact to him the incident had been a pleasant interlude.

As for me, the last of the family, my luck began at birth. Mother often told me of the scene. The doctor said to her, 'I think you have four boys, Mrs. Thomas?' 'Yes, yes . . . and I suppose this is another,' she replied in a resigned tone. 'Well, this is a little girl.' Whereupon my mother jumped up excitedly, crying, 'Let me see her, let me see her!' And it was only by swift appliances on the doctor's part that her life was saved. So from the very first I have never had the feeling of being an 'unwanted female'.

II

Ups and Downs

A SETTLED income has its attractions possibly, but it can never be the fun of an unsettled one. My father was on the Stock Exchange, and wavered between great affluence and extreme poverty. Neither he nor mother had a saving or economical disposition, but lived happily always, neither elated by wealth nor depressed by the lack of it.

We children were never aware of any money troubles, if such they could be called, for they made little difference to us. At no time were we allowed to spread our butter too thick. If things were going well, my father had no thought of enlarging his establishment or otherwise incurring bothers. His idea was that we should all enjoy ourselves a bit more along the old lines. When a shrinkage came we didn't notice much deprivation, or if we did it was put down to the weather. An oft-repeated family slogan was, 'Blessed is he that expecteth nothing, for he shall not be disappointed'. This happy-go-lucky attitude to life may be immoral from one point of view, but I have found it an excellent preparation for the continual uncertainties of my own lot.

An indulgence that mother often permitted herself was a drive in Hyde Park. Not far from us was a 'Jobbing Stable', which provided us with a victoria and a sprucely dressed red-faced old coachman named Henry. He would dash up at 2 o'clock, flicking his whip, and mother and I, all beautifully dressed, would get in, and be driven round among all the other carriages. How dull the saloon cars of to-day seem to me in comparison! Sometimes the Princess of Wales would pass us in the Row. I suppose I looked eager and excited and very young to be there, for once she smiled on me.

Now my father's pleasures took another direction. Not much more than a boy himself (for he married at the age of twenty-three) he loved cricket and all its social accompaniments. When money was plentiful he would take the boys, and often mother and me as well, in a wagonette to a cricket match, and give us all a big lunch, and invite any cricketers home to supper. Mother had a kind of fixed idea of a spread at home, no matter where we had been, so that we were always glad to get back. I don't think she intended it exactly, but this certainty of a cheerful meal, even when it could not be expensive, on our return home had a subtle influence on us.

When there was no outing possible, we played cricket in our back garden, and broke windows frequently. Each smash was a joy to me, because I loved to watch the glazier at his miraculous job. He always gave me a lump of putty which I made into dolls' cups and saucers, and snakes for Barnholt.

Among the many cricketers coming and going there was one who was so constantly staying with us that I looked on him as a kind of uncle. But we always called him by his full name, Charlie Absalom, so that I thought it was one word. He was a well-known cricketer of the time, and played I think for England against Australia. His travelling-kit was extremely simple, and he used to say that his packing up was done in two movements—gathering up his night-shirt with one hand and aiming it into his portmanteau wherever that happened to be. His jolly face made up for the fierceness of his black beard, which I fancy he cultivated on the model of Grace.

Of course Charlie Absalom played cricket with the boys and me in the back garden, gave me underhands when he bowled and easy catches when he batted (not that I caught them), and broke his due share of windows. I can hear his cheery voice calling out, 'Coosh! there goes another!' Mother never scolded when anything whatever was broken. As she justly remarked, 'People don't break things on purpose, and if you blame them they get nervous, and are more likely to break more.' And she was far too sensible to suppose that you can play cricket properly with half your mind engaged in fearing what the ball may break.

Some of the highest spots of my childhood were those sunny

Saturday afternoons when my father came home early with the word 'Kew' on his lips. Mother would throw aside any other plan, we all got ready in a trice, and trooped off in a body to the station at Canonbury. We did not make for the Gardens, as you might suppose, but always for the walk along the river bank to Richmond. This was wilder than the Gardens, allowing greater freedom of enterprise. Here were giant chestnut-trees, and competition in collecting the nuts. Whenever I pick up one to-day it brings back to me with its glossy lustre those rapturous afternoons. On our left we had glimpses of the Gardens, separated from us by a moat, and on our right ran the river, gay with rowing-boats, and every now and then sending ashore the wash of a pleasure-steamer, making 'real waves'.

After our walk, doubled by our scampering to and fro, we were ready for tea in a Richmond shop, and home again by train, to count our spoils and have endless games of conkers.

Another occasional playground for us was Epping Forest. The whole region was familiar ground to my father and mother, for here they had lived, during one of the depressed financial times, for several years in a tiny cottage, actually within the forest. It bore the charming name of Little Monkhams, and is now replaced by a row of villas. Little it certainly was, and I have often wondered how we all got in. Here the three youngest of us were born. Mother had a notion that it was improper to consult a doctor until the actual crisis, and Charles, who arrived unexpectedly at Christmas, was all but dead before the doctor could be fetched. The cottage was not only far from other habitations but was of the most primitive kind. Once, in a thunderstorm, the front windows blew out on to the lawn. Mother thought this very funny. But she must have been glad when a stroke of better fortune enabled us to move into the ample house in Canonbury.

An old married servant of ours, a Mrs. Pearce, lived at Theydon Bois, and used to welcome us at her cottage whenever we could come. She regaled us with milk from her own cow, with butter of her own make, and hot scones for tea.

A scamper in the Forest was the chief item in the programme, and on one occasion, still dark in my memory, we all set out in the usual style—the boys and I with Mrs. Pearce's little girl running ahead among the trees, while mother and Mrs. Pearce came on behind at a slow pace. Stopping to gather some grasses I forgot the others, and when I looked up was dismayed to see Charles just disappearing round a turn in the path some way on. I called out and ran as fast as my little legs would carry me, but I was only six years old and had little hope of catching them up. However, I still ran and tried to shout at the same time till I came to a place where the path divided. Which to take? I tried one a little way . . . and then ran back and tried the other. Then I found yet another path. Then I screamed and ran wildly this way and that. But there was dead silence, and on all sides the dark depths of the forest. Then the awful truth dawned on me that I was *lost*. Why are children told the story of the Babes in the Wood? With this in mind, I prepared to die. I lay down and waited for the birds to cover me with leaves. My hopeless misery is as vivid to me as if it had happened yesterday. I don't know how long I lay thus, but it cannot have been more than a quarter of an hour. I had not really strayed far from the main path, and I was soon found. The indescribable joy of hearing mother's voice calling me! I rushed to her, burbling out incoherences, but she never knew, no one ever knew, what it had been like. The glorious old forest is near my home to-day and I love to visit it, but its depths always hold a sinister flavour for me.

During the winter there were few recreations, however well off we might be. We all hated 'parties', because it meant being fixed into best clothes and behaving properly instead of having a good romp. The boys used to go to the theatre and music halls. The latter sounded rather dull, but mother explained that they were not dull, only not very nice. However, it made no difference to me what they were like, since I was never allowed to go even to a theatre. Tom and Charles were our theatre-tasters, and they went to see everything that Irving did. Charles told me the story of *The Bells*, which frightened me a bit, but I never tired of *Hamlet*, and watching Charles, who was tall and dark and thin, striding about the house in imitation of Irving, with his chin stuck out, bidding me go to a nunnery, or stabbing an imaginary Polonius hiding behind the red dining-room curtains. Bernardo, Francisco, Horatio, what good mouthfuls they made! 'Stand and unfold yourself', I would shout, and 'Get thee to bed, Francisco.' Our old family volume of the Tragedies, with Kenny Meadows's illustrations, still opens at *Hamlet*.

When the mood took us we would push back the dining room table and act charades. The main point was to appear different from usual, putting on a bonnet of mother's, a pillow to make us fat, my father's top hat or overcoat. When other amusements failed we fell back on games. Mother possessed a marvellous box, replete with everything necessary. It opened out in compartments, revealing chessmen fixed on to holders, draughts, bezique-cards, cribbage-board, dominoes, and packs of ordinary cards. I can't remember when I didn't know how to play chess, not to mention all the other games.

My father liked a rubber of whist, and I was taught to make a fourth in my tenderest years. The scoring, rapidly muttered by my father, was quite beyond me, but I drew a certain comfort from hearing him announce that honours were easy. I dealt with extreme slowness, hugging the pack tightly, dreading the disgrace of a misdeal. The others would sit back and wait with ostentatious patience until I had finished. A few clear rules I clung to, such as 'never revoke', 'third player play his highest'. This was a sore trial to me if I held the ace of trumps. The glory of having it was balanced by the pain of parting with it. What I liked was to hoard my trumps as a surprise for the end. Dym, who had an unaccountable way of knowing what cards I had, used to impress on me that there were only two excuses for not returning your partner's lead —sudden illness, or not having any of the suit. And mother, gazing at the ceiling while I was hesitating, would refer casually to the 'thousand men now driving cabs in London because they wouldn't lead trumps'. So, as you will guess, the glory

of winning a trick was quite wiped out by the misery of having
to lead. I did my best to avoid Dym as a partner, owing to his
horrible questions at the end: 'My dear child, didn't you *see*
my call for trumps?' My father or Tom was the best partner,
for he would let bygones be bygones, and had no hopes of
improving me.

In spite of these alleviations the London winters were long
and dark and cold. Fogs in those days were far worse than
the mild affairs we have to-day—far blacker and more solid.
The boys liked a frost so as to get some skating in Regent's
Park or at Hendon, or even some sliding at Finsbury Park.
But I never had the courage to try, and hated the cold. I think
mother felt the same, for she used to proclaim as soon as
October dawned: 'Now, children, remember, the month after
next the days will begin to lengthen.'

And of course lean times were vaguely felt by us all, however much the high spirits of our parents hid them. One day
I heard my father say to mother, 'Never mind, Mary, whatever happens you and I are in the same boat—so nothing
matters.' I knew then that something must be going wrong,
but his words, and the pleasure in mother's face, pushed deep
down into me a sense of happy security.

Two incidents during such lean periods caused more merriment than distress. One autumn afternoon a friend dropped
in to tea, and, in the teeth of mother's increasing coolness of
manner, kept staying on and on. It grew dusk, but still no
signs of departure. At last mother announced in firm tones
that she was very fond of sitting in the gloaming and watching
the lamplighter dodging from side to side. With that she rose
markedly, adding that she did not wish to force her friends
to engage in such simple pleasures. Whereupon the friend,
with a nervous giggle and a 'You are so funny, Mrs. Thomas',
reached the door and went, never suspecting that our gas had
been cut off by the Company.

At another time of poverty my mother had bought a pair
of kippers for supper, to regale my father after the children
were in bed. He managed to get some stout to add to the feast.

Just as all was ready who should arrive but Aunt Polly, 'only for a minute, dear'. But the savoury smell was too much for her, and she consented to stay to supper. The nakedness of the land was only too clear to her, but instead of declaring (as poor mother had to) that kippers disagreed with her, she did her good deed by pouring the small remains of the stout into a bottle 'against another time'. Alas, she must needs select the bottle in which was an iron ration of whisky, hoarded by us in case of illness. Among Polly's many shortcomings this particular folly rankled longest in mother's mind.

I suppose it must have been during a lean year, when we were devoid even of servants, that my father would inaugurate some lark. One afternoon he came home early and suggested that it was just the sort of day for making toffee. The boys sprang to the idea, but mother hesitated, as she didn't know quite how to make it. But when my father said that he knew all about it because they had made it at school once, we all followed him in a glad rush to the kitchen. Barnholt was sent to the grocer close by for 'a pound of his worst butter'. All grins, Barnholt flew forth on his errand. The grocer was annoyed at such a request, but, as Barnholt pointed out to him, if he had a best butter he must have a worst. Not seeing the obvious retort to this, he grumblingly served out a pound of something which my father declared to exceed his worst expectations. Meanwhile mother had brought out sugar, and, after much searching of cupboards, some treacle. All was put in a saucepan and Dym was placed to stir it over the fire, while Charles measured out a tablespoonful of vinegar. My part was to get in every one's way and ask why each thing was done. My father's explanation of the vinegar was peculiar, having some strange reference to the Franco-Prussian War. When mother had greased some flat tins the mixture was poured into them, and we had to wait a bit till it was set. I can't remember what it tasted like, but I know we were all in a glorious mess.

Another time it was a Welsh rabbit that my father had a mind for, and a syndicate was again formed for its creation. In this case the Franco-Prussian ingredient was a little beer.

My father did the careful stirring this time, and two of the boys got round his legs making toast. Mother hovered around, shaking her head, prophesying indigestion and the doctor. But she ate her share and wished it had been bigger.

The best of these impromptu feasts was a positive shoal of sprats that my father came home with one evening. 'They're practically alive,' said he, 'and they were almost giving them away in Farringdon Market. Now, Mary, bring out your biggest frying-pan and some dripping, make up the fire, and you boys put the plates to warm. You shall have some fish on them before you know where you are.' And lo, it was so. There was a sizzling and a tossing, and soon the crisp little fish were tumbling on to our outstretched plates, while mother was cutting bread and butter as fast as she could. I have had elegantly dressed sole at a grand dinner, salmon straight from the Dart, trout fresh from a Welsh stream, and perch that I caught myself in a Canadian river, but no fish has ever had the magic quality of those sprats 'given away' in London and cooked by my father.

III

Round the Year

A FEW definite occasions throughout the year were cele-
brated whatever our circumstances or whatever the
weather.

The earliest of these has now all but died out. February 14th
comes and goes unnoticed. But St. Valentine was a reality to
us. Why this Christian Martyr should be connected with love
affairs no one seems to know. Probably his feast is a survival
of a pagan one in spring, like the famous Furry in Cornwall.
As children we took full advantage of it, and spent our pocket-
money in buying valentines and sending them (always anony-
mously, that was *de rigueur*) to cousins and friends. The little
shops near us, and the stationers in Upper Street, used to fill
their windows with the regulation cards. Indeed they were
more than cards, for the better ones consisted of shallow cardboard boxes, decorated with paper lace surrounding a coloured
device of forget-me-not, or a picture of a boy and girl bowing
to one another, with a verse of sentimental nature below. Some
contained a present of a pair of gloves or a purse or a tie. All
of us 'had a valentine'—a sweetheart of some kind, whose name
we kept as a dead secret, and there was much fun trying to
guess the senders.

In later years I tried in vain to buy a valentine, even going
to Whiteley's for the purpose, and reminding the shop-walker
with some acerbity that they called themselves 'universal pro-
viders'. Upon this he became facetious and I thought it best to
say no more.

The boat race was the most absorbing topic of the spring.
For some unknown reason we were all violently Cambridge.
So much so that I fancied there was something definitely disgraceful about Oxford. Long before the great day people
showed their colours, nearly every horse wore a piece of ribbon,

and little errand-boys came to open blows in the street as to the respective merits of the Universities. When I was pursued by cries of 'Yah! dirty Cambridge!' I felt like planting a blow myself. The journey to the river was a fairly long one, and when the tide obliged the race to be early the boys seemed to get up in the middle of the night. In spite of my intense interest in the race, I never went to see it. I never went to any entertainment, not even to the Agricultural Hall, where the boys used to go continually.

All Fools' day had to be observed at school or outside the house somewhere, for the family was too alert to be taken in. We knew all the time-honoured errands for pigeons' milk, strap-oil, fresh salt, and plaice without spots. Nothing would induce us to move a step to 'come and look' at anything until noon on April 1st. But we enjoyed recounting our triumphs at tea in the evening, and also our defeats, for after all a really clever defeat could be saved up and tried on some one else next year.

None of us, so far as I remember, ever went to the Derby, but the race was a great subject of talk, and my father always got up a family sweepstake. It seemed such a serious occasion that I had a vague idea that it had started in Old Testament times.

Bank holidays were much the same for Londoners as they are now—a day for remaining at home or for getting as far away as possible. In this matter we divided. Mother and I did the one, and my father and the boys the other. They used to start off by an early train, and take one of their colossal walks into the country, or else go fishing in the River Lea. Then off went the servants somewhere (probably to Hampstead Heath) for the entire day. Mother and I stayed at home to enjoy what she called 'the freedom of the wild ass', with no lessons, no proper meals, no duty walks, and above all no chance of callers. As soon as the boys had gone I used to watch for the big wagonettes full of children going off to Chingford or Epping for the day. They used to sing and wave flags, and I waved to them. After this the neighbourhood became sepulchral— 'silence like a poultice came to heal the blows of sound'.

Mother must have been very clever in thinking up jolly things to do, for I can never remember feeling dull or out of it when the boys went off anywhere. She had the knack of vicarious enjoyment, and we used to live through what the others were probably doing: 'Now they are having their sandwiches', 'Now I expect they have caught some fish', 'Perhaps Charles has done a sketch'.

After tea it was my cue to watch at the window for the return of the wagonettes. I must say I took a grim pleasure in the peevish tones that came from the tired children, and the scoldings of the mothers, not to mention the lack of song and flag-waving. Our next business was to lay the cloth for supper and make a big spread for the hungry home-comers. At one such evening meal mother exclaimed, 'How well you look, Dym!' The others smiled in a gratified way and spoke of the health-giving properties of country walking. It was not till many days had passed that they told her how Dym had fallen into the river and barely been saved from drowning. He had been taken to an inn, put into a hot bath, rubbed down, wrapped in blankets while his clothes were dried, and given whisky. No wonder, as he was hurried home as fast as possible, that he looked a bit rosy. He had a delicate chest, and had once been at death's door, while we crept about the house, alarmed at the arrival of a second doctor.

Strange as it seems to-day, when excursions are so cheap, a London family often went without any 'summer holiday' at all. There were certainly 'excursion trains', but they meant all that was horrible: long and unearthly hours, packed carriages, queer company, continual shuntings aside and waiting for regular trains to go by, and worst of all the contempt of decent travellers. We had a little rhyme about them which ended:

> *Grown old and rusted, the boiler busted*
> *And smashed the excursion train.*

So for a large family a trip to the sea-side was an expensive affair. In the years when we did not go to Cornwall, therefore we either bore the heat of London or had a fortnight at

Walton-on-the-Naze. It looks very near on the map, but it was quite a business to get there. Liverpool Street was never the easiest of stations to start with, and then we had to change at Colchester. I can still see my mother's anguished face at this junction, as she got us all out, counted our many parcels, went to see if the heavy luggage had been shifted, made repeated in-quiries (so as to make sure) as to the right platform, and then packed us all in again for the final lap. As a rule, my father could only get away for week-ends, when he and Charlie Absalom or an uncle would come by steamer.

The cabman at Walton knew us, and the landlady at the lodgings welcomed us, and all the troubles of the journey were quickly forgotten as we rushed to greet the sea. Although the place has now been improved beyond recognition with hotels, restaurants, and new types of boarding-houses, the sea and its attractions are just the same. Buckets and spades are the same pattern and colour, sand-castles and fortifications no grander or stronger than ours, donkeys just as recalcitrant. Indeed, we had one advantage over the children of to-day, for no one had discovered that continual paddling was bad for you, so we were barefoot all the time, in and out of the water, scrambling over breakwaters, fishing for crabs, collecting shells and stones, and screwing our toes into the wriggly sand.

At an ill-starred moment mother decided that I was old enough to bathe like the boys. She selected for her experiment a nice pool beside a long, low rock, discreetly far from the main beach. I was quite excited at the idea of doing something like the boys, consented to be stripped, and paddled boldly forward. Mother thought that all she need do was to carry on with her sewing, and throw me words of encouragement. 'Sit down, darling. Splash about a little. Go a little farther in. Don't mind getting wet all over. It won't hurt you. . . .' But there I stood, not quite knee-deep, fixed, with a safety-first idea. Now mother had no use for obstinacy, and thinking me no more than obstinate she laid aside her sewing with some sharpness, walked along the rock, stooped and seized my readily outstretched hand, at the same time giving me a little jerk forward and downward into the water. Aware now that my last moments were approaching, I pulled my hardest. Mother's foot slipped, and flop! she went headlong into the pool. Her summer frock, a mass of flounces and ribbons, her beautiful wide hat . . . they hardly bear thinking about. She managed to dress me somehow, to gather up her sewing, and walk back to our lodgings, dripping water all the way, adding greatly to the cheerfulness of the 'front'.

When my father was told of it he said I ought to be punished, 'because a child should be taught to recognize a disaster when it happens'. However, he added, 'You punish her, dear. It will come better from you.' As this was his well-known method of getting out of something he hated doing, they both laughed. The only upshot was that mother was promised a new dress, I had a big hug from my father on the quiet, and my bathing lessons were postponed.

To vary our shore pleasures we used to strike inland, and were in real country at once, for there were no 'respectable' roads and villas surrounding the place. Frinton lane was a lonely walk, almost alarmingly so, with its trees overhead. To me it was the 'shady lane', down which Tom and Jane met their death in the poem from eating 'scarlet berries'. Mother's horror of deadly nightshade was only equalled by her fear of green paint. The mushrooms and blackberries we brought in added pleasantly to our landlady's limited cuisine. Her apple tarts and puddings were really clove confections flavoured with apple.

When the boys were off on some long wet-weather tramp, mother and I stayed in our lodgings. She would sketch something from the window, or else do a bit of necessary sewing. She hated sewing so much that she generally stood to do it. I have inherited both the hatred and the posture, but am still puzzled at the reason for standing. Does it get it over sooner? At home, mother coped in a simple way with the eternal mending required for the family. She hired an extremely old maid to spend every Friday with us. There she sat all day, at a little table in the kitchen window, mending. She would never lend her scissors, not for a moment, and if I asked her to 'button me up' she would do it very slowly, and say, 'Patience is a virtue.' This sounded like a text, but I believe it was a hideous thought entirely her own.

While the boys were off, and mother busy, I was completely happy with a wooden stool on four legs, padded with red velvet. It was a treasure belonging to the landlady, who brought it out for me specially, with the request that the young gentlemen should not sit on it. Mother, knowing the young gentlemen, hid it always until they were out of the way, and then I had such glory with it that it compensated for my being left at home. It became in turn a table, a bed, a funeral coach, a train, a station, a pirate vessel for stealing mother's brushes or cotton, and oftenest of all it was Bucephalus, on which I careered about the room, conquering country after country. The boys returned all too soon.

Back again in London we had to settle down to a long stretch of 'everydayness'. October is bound to be enjoyable always, but November meant fogs, trees bared before they had time to get red and gold, and perhaps 'doing without a fire' because it was not quite cold enough. The one excitement to be certain of was the Lord Mayor's Show, coinciding with the Prince of Wales's birthday, and a school holiday. Needless to say, I never saw the Show myself. The boys always went, and came home full of their struggles with the crowd and their prowess in elbowing their way to the front. It seemed to me something like the way Cinderella went to the ball, from their description of the coach. They always brought home for me a little book, that opened out to nearly a yard of coloured pictures, displaying all the features of the Show. This was called 'A Penny Panorama of the Lord Mayor's Show', and the name pleased me so much that for days afterwards I would go about the house pretending to be a hawker, crying:

> *Buy my Panorama, my penny Panorama,*
> *My penny Panorama of the Lord Mayor's Show.*

Mere river-side excursions were indulged in at any time, the steamer trip to Greenwich and back being the usual one. For the boys, of course, not me. All I culled from them was a new chant for my play: 'Ease her, back her, stop her', and the longer instructions: 'When in danger with no room to turn, ease her, stop her, go astern', and 'When you see three lights ahead, port your helm and show your red'.

Nowadays it is difficult to realize that no Christmas preparations were made until the week before the day itself. All our excitement was packed into a short space. The boys were on holiday, and all over the place. Mother was mostly in the kitchen, presiding over mincemeat and puddings. I was set to clean currants, squeeze lemons, and cut up candied peel. Barnholt lent a hand at chopping the suet, but kept making raids on the lumps of sugar tucked away in the candied peel, which he assured me were very hard and nasty in the mincemeat, but had no ill effects on him.

Tom and Dym kept going to Upper Street to get stationery, cards, and presents from the shops. Charles spent his time in painting home-made Christmas cards. Midday dinner was a noisy buzz of comparing notes on the morning's doings, and having a look at what Charles had produced. The afternoons were generally given up to the preparation of our annual play. It fell to Tom to devise the plot, and to Charles, the Bully Bottom of the family, fell nearly everything else. He took the part of the villain or the comic washerwoman, and kept thinking up ideas for improving the parts of the others. He taught me how to act when I wasn't speaking, how to listen with agitation, how to do 'by-play', how to swoon, and once even how to die. Dym was usually the hero, a bit stiff, but always dignified. Barnholt had to be given a part with little to say, because, however willing, he could not be relied on to remember the words, or improvise other ones. He would be a coachman or a footman, or perhaps only the scene-shifter. What he really loved was to be the policeman, coming in at the crisis with a "Ere, what's all this?', pulling out his note-book, wetting his thumb, and taking people's addresses. He knew his stuff for this perfectly, but it wouldn't always fit into melodrama.

Tom, to my great comfort, was prompter, and saved me from many a breakdown when I was swamped with nervousness. I didn't actually forget my words, but I should have done if Tom hadn't stood by smiling at me behind the screen.

Christmas Eve was the day we liked best. The morning was a frenzied rush for last rehearsals, last posting of cards, last buying of presents. My father came home early, laden with parcels. The tea-table was resplendent with bon-bons (crackers), sweets, and surprise cakes with icing on the top and threepenny-bits inside. The usual 'bread and butter first' rule was set aside, and we all ate and talked and laughed to our heart's content.

Then followed the solemn ascent to the study for the play. The boys had borrowed chairs from the bedrooms, and placed them in two rows : the front (stalls) for father, mother, and any aunt, uncle, or visitor who happened to be there, and the back (pit) for the servants, who attended with much gigglement.

Personally I was thankful when this nerve-strain was over, and we all crowded down into the breakfast-parlour. Here, earlier in the day, mother and I had arranged the presents—a little pile for each, and we all fell upon them with delight. We were never fussed up with a Christmas tree or stockings or make-believe about Santa Claus. Perhaps we were too hard-headed. Perhaps mother considered that waking up in the small hours to look at stockings was a bad beginning for an exciting day. As it was, we had nice time before bed for peeping into our new books, and gloating over all the fresh treasures.

Christmas Day itself followed a regular ritual. Service at St. Paul's was exactly the same as it is now, the same hymns and even the same decorations (knots of red velvet hung on the pillars). The post was the next excitement, and we displayed our cards on the mantelpiece. The traditional dinner of turkey and plum pudding and dessert was followed by a comatose afternoon, during which Barnholt cooked chestnuts incessantly on the bars of the grate, tossing them to us as they were done.

The evening festivities began with the ceremony of punch-making. This was always my father's special job, and he spread himself over it royally. Quantities of loaf sugar and lemons were assembled, and a very large glass jug. A kettle of water was on the fire. The lemon-juice and sugar were stirred together at the bottom of the jug, then a tumblerful each of rum and brandy were added. Carefully my father then filled the jug with boiling water. Carefully, because once the boiling water smashed the jug, and everything splashed over the dining-room table. He laughed and called for all the ingredients over again. 'We've lost the punch,' said he, 'we needn't also lose a bit of our lives by crying over it.'

IV

Sailing Near the Wind

'NOTHING peculia happened to-day.' Such is the entry again and again in my first diary, a large 'Renshaw' for 1876, presented by my father, filled in with anxious care, and preserved even till to-day. The main 'care' was that events being so few I was driven to record even the fact of going to bed. My outside amusements were mainly pale reflections of what the boys told me about theirs. The Agricultural Hall was within easy reach of us, and I wondered what the boys found so attractive in a place with such a name. Of course I was never allowed to go there myself, but gathered that it was not all concerned with farming and cattle and pigs. At one time a man named Weston used to walk round and round the Hall to see how long he could keep it up. This seemed to me a foolish game, but the boys liked to watch him, especially when he had ten minutes' rest, and fell asleep in the arms of his attendants.

Far more exciting to me were the accounts the boys brought home from the Polytechnic. The name had a gayer sound, and here there was a Diving-Bell. You went into a little room inside a big bell, and were let down into water. So they said, but of course I didn't believe it. However, it sounded a delightful take-in, and I used to shout about the house, 'This way for the Diving-Bell.' Dym took the trouble to show me, with the aid of a tumbler, a rag, and a pail of water, how the diving-bell worked. I was amazed, but still unbelieving that people would trust themselves to go under water just because a rag in a tumbler managed somehow to keep dry.

Strange as it seems I was never taken to anything more exciting than a picture gallery, not even to a pantomime at Christmas. Not even to the Tower or the Crystal Palace or Madame Tussaud's—places to which the boys had to conduct country cousins, with profuse grumblings. I suppose it was their expressed boredom with such excursions that reconciled me to staying at home. However, whenever there was any game afoot actually in the house or garden I was allowed to join in. Some of these were kept secret, lest they should be labelled 'naughty', but I cannot remember that we were ever punished severely. An occasional putting in the corner for me, and a threatened 'slippering' of the boys by my father if they were too noisy—these were the usual penalties. When one of the boys had really annoyed mother, she would address him, as 'Sir', and send him to have his hair cut. This does not sound so bad as it in fact was. Our only available hairdresser had a strange habit of keeping a customer waiting for a half to three-quarters of an hour. There was nothing to do but stare at a fern and a picture of Cromwell sitting at his daughter's death-bed.

A kind of family 'common law', an unwritten code, seemed to have existed from the beginning of time and was accepted as inevitable by us all. One rule was that one went to bed the moment the word was said, without argument or plea. Another was that one ate up everything on one's plate. Tom once had to finish the mustard which he had too liberally taken, and I can still recall the swelling in my throat as I bolted my last piece of blancmange. Another law was that we must never be rude to servants. Beyond these there was nothing criminal, except perhaps taking mother's scissors for our private ends.

So infrequent were my own punishments that I recall vividly the two occasions when I deserved them and obtained them. One morning I was bored with my lessons, looked round for some little drama, and proclaimed myself thirsty. Already I suppose I had discovered that a mother can require resistance to hunger, but not to thirst. 'Run downstairs then, dear, and ask cook to give you a glass of water.' Down I went, and after a decent delay returned with the report that cook had refused to give it to me. Now, thought I, for some fireworks. Alas! mother didn't even send for the cook or institute inquiries, or appear disturbed at all. She said, 'Write in your diary, "I told a lie to-day".' There was no escaping it, my beautiful diary had to be thus disfigured, staring at me. And to this day I think the punishment was excessive.

The other disgrace was still more memorable because it was a strain, and the only one, between me and my father. Charles was reading Hans Andersen: I wanted the book, asked for it, fussed for it, and finally broke into tears. This brought my father into the room, and I hoped for the best. But he became dreadfully serious, led me upstairs, and administered a whipping. Then he explained that it is as bad for a girl to cry for what she wants as for a boy to plant a blow. I might cry a very little if I was badly hurt, but never, never must I cry just to get something.

Adventures of a kind that were not forbidden mainly because mother didn't know about them were plentiful enough, and usually carried out in the back garden. One boy would dare another to some perilous act, while I was a delighted looker-on, half dreading and half hoping for the worst. An acacia-tree stood at the end of the garden. Into this the boys would climb and then swing themselves over into the street— a considerable drop. Another feat was to walk along the top of the high, narrow wall, endowed with bits of glass. The most dangerous of all was climbing round a ledge, some two inches wide, that ran along the house over the area. The boy who attempted this had to flatten himself, spread out his arms, and press his palms against the wall. This particular part of the back premises was invisible from any window, and was therefore chosen when we were 'sailing near the wind', as my father called any near approach to the sinful.

I was merely an onlooker, but was allowed on one occasion to join in an open-air smoking concert in these back premises. Barnholt had been sent out to buy some 'jumbles'— a thin kind of gingerbread about the size of a saucer, so crisp that it curled up. I was given a jumble, a front seat, and (bliss beyond words!) a pipe to put in my mouth. All was in train when who should casually open the back door but mother. . . . I remember that my jumble fell in fragments at my feet and that the rest of the incident was a storm of scolding that I should dare to put a pipe in my mouth. The crime had only been omitted from the ten commandments because not even Moses could imagine that a little girl should so disgrace herself. And so on. It lasted a long time. But how I did regret not having had one bite of my jumble.

'How I wish I were a boy!' Mother caught me saying this aloud one day, and promptly told me that this was a wicked thought. She did not go on to give a reason, but merely insisted that it was splendid to be a girl, and with such exuberant enthusiasm that I was quite convinced. My father's slogan was that boys should go everywhere and know everything, and that a girl should stay at home and know nothing. Often the boys must have been sorry for me, and one day when I exclaimed, 'How lovely it must be to go on the top of a bus!', Dym first laughed at the idea, and then suddenly said, 'I say, Barney, let's take her.' Barnholt, of course, was only too ready, and I rushed to get my things on before something could happen to stop us. If I had been asked to a royal ball I couldn't have been more excited.

Inside a bus I had often been with mother when we went to Shoolbred's or Peter Robinson's for a morning's shopping. The bus was a box lined with blue velvet, made to carry five each side, of whom mother declared that the fattest always sat next her and half on her, for she was very small. No air got in, except when the door was opened, for the little windows admitted only some so-called light. Straw on the floor, designed to keep our feet warm, was apt to get very wet and dirty. When the bus started the door was firmly shut, the conductor remaining outside with no visible means of support. Presently he would let down the top of the door, put his head in, and ask, 'Any for the Angel?'—or whatever the next stage happened to be. Then fares were handed up to him (no tickets were used), and he made a mark with a stumpy pencil on a yellow sheet. I knew what this sheet was called, because all I could amuse myself with during the journey was to read the directions beseeching the passengers to see that their fares were 'duly registered on the waybill at the door'. We stopped anywhere, for plenty of passengers rather than rapid progress was the main idea. I reckon that the journey from Islington to the West End took a good deal over an hour. Wedged as we were, it was impossible to see anything out of the tiny windows, and the journey was sheer boredom. What with the lack of air, the jerks of the frequent stops, and the jolting over the stone-paved roads, I was usually too ill to stay the course, and we had to get out some distance before our required shop.

Mysterious as was the mode of attachment of the conductor, the means of getting on to the top was still more so. From the glimpses I had from inside people disappeared bit by bit, their boots last. Of course no woman ever went up. And now, here was I, going to do it myself!

I rushed up again to the study, all dressed, and Dym surveyed me and said I would do. My outdoor clothes in winter never varied: a hat of real sealskin that stood all weathers and could not wear out, neither could it blow off, for it was fastened round my chin by elastic; my warmth was secured by a 'cross-over'—a strip of tartan about two yards long that crossed over in front and fastened behind, leaving my arms free. The worst worry in going out were my boots, which came far above the ankle with endless buttons that needed a hook to do them up.

Dym decided that it would be best for us to walk to the little side street not far away, where the 'Favourite' buses began their journeys. Here we were able to make the ascent at leisure. Dym went up first, then hung down and pointed out the tiny ledges on which I had to put my feet, stretching out his hands to pull me up, while Barnholt fetched up the rear in case I slipped. On the top was what they called the knifeboard—a raised partition along the middle, with seats each side. How people stuck on to them I couldn't imagine. But the boys had better designs: they scrambled down on to the seat in front, by the driver, and got me there too. 'Come along, Missy,' said the driver, who was just settling himself for his journey, and I was safely tucked in between him and Dym, with Barnholt on his other side.

How powerful the horse looked from this point of view,

how jolly to hear the chuckings and whoas, and to see the whip flourished about, but only gently touching the horse. 'I never whips old Rosy,' the driver told me. 'She's been with me six years and knows what I want. I use the whip like chatting to her.' How pitiable were all the people on foot! How contemptible the passengers who went inside! Barnholt, as look-out man, kept calling my attention to things in the shops, and to people doing mysterious jobs in first-floor windows. One room was a nursery, where a boy was riding on a rocking-horse, and in one garden we passed there was a swing with a boy going very high.

We feared to go the whole length of our twopenny ride in case we should be late for tea, so we asked the driver to pull up for us. In my haste to show him how well I could get off by jumping down to Dym in front I fell right into the muddy street. But no harm was done, and the boys picked me up, and we ran home as fast as we could and slipped in at the back door. There was no hiding my mud, and 'Wherever have you been?' cried mother. 'Oh, just for a run with the boys, and I fell.' This was true enough to pass my conscience. Dym was nonplussed, but Barnholt immediately took up the tale of a fine new shop where they sold cricket-bats and bags and things, and how he had thought it better not to spend the shilling Uncle Alfred had given him. On this wave of virtue my muddy dress was forgotten, and we went into tea with no further questions asked.

One morning in the winter holidays I heard a plan being propounded in the study that called for nerve, and promised well. It was one of Charles's bright ideas, and Barnholt would gladly have joined in. 'No,' said Charles, 'you would laugh and spoil all.' 'I promise not to,' pleaded Barnholt, but Charles maintained, and rightly I think, that to know what was going on in Barnholt's head was worse even than his laughter.

So the serious-looking Dym was appealed to, and after much persuasion agreed to come along. Now Charles had discovered the position of four girls' schools in the nieghbourhood. He had seen the brass plates with 'Establishment for

Young Ladies'. His idea, so he said, was to call for a prospectus. Dym saw no objection to this, and off they started, but Barnholt and I suspected that Charles had further designs, and we waited for their return with eagerness.

They were a long time away, but returned at last highly satisfied and letting off their suppressed laughter. They told us that at the first school the servant fetched them a prospectus. But Charles looked at it for a moment severely and then asked if he might see the head mistress about a certain point. The servant went away, and Dym was all for fleeing quite quickly, but while he hesitated the servant returned and ushered them into a drawing-room all sofas and cushions, for impressing parents. Again Dym suggested a breakaway. Again he was prevented. In sailed the head mistress all smiles and graciousness, and bade them be seated. With the utmost coolness Charles made a little speech to the effect that Mamma was not very well, and had sent them to inquire whether there would be a vacancy for next term, that they had a little sister, a most promising child, who was about to begin the third declension in Latin, and was of a sweet disposition. Poor Dym nervously made murmurs of agreement in the background, and wrote down name and address at the lady's request on her fine notepaper. Meanwhile the bell had been rung, and cake and currant wine were brought in. Charles became more imaginative under their influence, and the boys departed in the best odour.

At the other three schools they had very much the same experience, except that Dym, by Charles's advice, gave a made-up name and address. The refreshment varied from cake to biscuits and figs, and in the last case the wine was sherry. Perhaps it was as well that this was the last. Barnholt was worried to think of the cake and wine he had missed, but I was greatly set up at being described as promising, although Charles took care to tell me that he didn't mean anything he said.

Unfortunately a week later, when we had forgotten all about the affair, the first head mistress called on mother, who knew nothing of what had happened. She was rather bewildered, and disclaimed having sent any message. 'What is all this, Molly?'

said she to me, as I was trying to be unobserved in a corner. But I never knew anything that the boys did, and looked quite puzzled.

'Your sons are very nice mannered,' said the head mistress, 'but to tell the truth I had the gravest doubts about their message.' Then with laughter and apologies the scene closed in good humour, for mother had the wit to add, 'If ever I do want to send Molly to school I shall know which one to choose.'

In some escapades I was actually useful. November 5th fell one year on a half-holiday. Tom was away at school, Dym was staying at school to play fives, Barnholt for once had no detention, so we three youngest were free for anything. Naturally Charles had an idea. 'Why not make a guy and go round the streets with it? We could disguise ourselves so that nobody would know us . . . do let's.'

Barnholt then suggested that I could be the guy because I was so small. Indeed the boys often used to give me a chair-ride by clasping their own wrists for a seat while I steadied myself on it by putting my arms round their necks. But Charles had seen in the back kitchen an old cane chair without a back, and he thought this would be better. Mother was intending to pay some calls and was safely in her bedroom getting her things on. So we crept downstairs and told the servants what we wanted to do. These servants had been with us simply for ever and joined in any of our larks with enthusiasm. A guy going by was exciting enough to them, but to dress one was a joyous break to a dull afternoon. They found the little chair, sat me in it, and draped the red cotton kitchen tablecloth round me. Meanwhile Barnholt had made paper cocked hats for us all and Charles provided us with black moustaches from the soot of a candle-flame. My plaid cross-over was pinned in a martial style over Barnholt's shoulder, and the housemaid lent Charles her black cape to make him look villainous. As I had my hands free the candle was put in one, and a tin box for contributions in the other. Charles wrote GUNPOWDER on a sheet of note-paper to place behind the tin. At last all was ready, and as soon as we heard mother close the front door we stole out at the back, staggering up the area steps with difficulty.

Making as quickly as possible for a side street we certainly attracted little attention that would distress us, but neither did we attract the pennies. Charles saw that we needed to make some kind of *noise*, and he started a hymn. This sounded so absurd in the street that Barnholt and I shook with laughing in trying to say that earth hath many a noble city. Well, we knew that laughter would be no use—we must look pathetic if we wanted pennies. Just as we were beginning to feel rather damped we heard the dismal strains of an organ-grinder. 'The very thing!' cried Charles, and we wobbled off in the direction of the sound. I can see now the broad grin of the man as he readily consented to our going along with him. Soon another brain-wave came over Charles, and he asked the man to help carry the chair while he himself had a try at grinding the organ. Of course Barnholt wanted to try too, and the man said they might take it in turns.

Then indeed success began. 'Tommy make room for your uncle' had new interest. Jaded hearers were astonished to find the well-known air first rendered by Charles as a funeral march, and then by Barnholt as a mad gallop. Windows were thrown open, and amid cries of 'poor little souls' pennies and halfpennies came hurtling down. I was placed on the ground while the coins were gathered up, and my tin box began to fill. After some of this triumphant proceeding, the organ-grinder became aware that we had only gone through two streets. He said he must get along faster, as he had to do his 'round'. This was a new idea to me, that he had a round like a milkman. But when I came to think of it I remembered that on regular days and at regular hours an organ-grinder would be heard in our road. People looked to see him, he said, and it would never do to disappoint them.

We had some trouble to get him to take the box of money. 'No, take it home to your por ma,' said he, and we had to explain that it was only a lark, and that 'por ma' wouldn't like it at all. So we settled matters by taking a penny each, which we turned into acid drops at a little shop at the corner. Fortunately it was now getting dusk, and we hoped to slip home without being seen by any one who knew us. As luck would have it we came full tilt on mother at the gate. She was so glad, however, to get home after a solid hour's calling ('aching behind the ears with being polite', as she described it) that she only laughed at our appearance and said, 'You naughty children, go and wash at once.' We were sensible enough not to mention the episode of the organ-grinder and the moneys received, let alone that the vicar had met us and dropped a whole sixpence into the box. We suspected that he recognized us, but he played the game and kept very grave.

Coloured paper decorations could not be bought in those days, but we used to make our own festoons by cutting alternate slits in a long strip of paper and pulling it out. One day I found Barnholt busy doing this, and fastening his festoons right across the study from corner to corner of the ceiling. He would not tell me what they were for, and was so darkly mysterious that my curiosity was whetted, especially as he hinted that he was to set fire to the paper at some great moment. On the floor I noticed that our specimens of Cornish stone had been piled on an upturned box. As soon as tea was over the boys hurried up to the study 'to do their work'. Knowing that something was afoot I followed them, but only after a decent interval so as to allay suspicion.

As I drew near to the study door I heard mournful strains of solemn chanting. I smelt something strong and strange, that I knew afterwards to be incense. In great fear I listened, and presently there were horrid cries as of some one in pain. Opening the door a few inches I caught sight of a dark room, lit only by a fire burning on the stones, three candles, and the festoons of paper which were waving half-burnt from above. I was too terrified to speak to the boys, who were stalking round the fire clothed in sheets, and waving their arms about. Suddenly Charles caught sight of me, pushed me back, and shut the door with the words, 'You mustn't come in. We are having druidical sacrifices and you'll tell.'

With bitter cries of 'I won't tell, oh, do let me in!' I had to go away and swallow my disappointment, sitting disconsolate on the stairs in the dark. Few things in life have given me such a sense of injury. Not only was I denied the fearful enjoyment of the human sacrifice, but I had been accused of being likely to *tell!* That was dead against the first law of the family. I don't think Charles really meant this. What he feared was my discovery that he had taken my big wax doll for the human victim. When I reached the door it must have been then melting on the altar. As if I should have minded! What was a doll in comparison to the treat that I had missed!

On coming downstairs I was greeted by mother's usual 'Well, dear, I suppose the boys are too hard at work to want you in the study?' 'Yes, mother,' I said, 'they are doing something out of Roman history.'

V

Up to Eleven

I'm six years old this very day,
And I can write and read,
And not to have my own way
Is very hard indeed.

THE boys had the advantage of me in going about, but I
had the advantage of them in not being sent to school.
Until my eleventh year I was saved from the stupefying
influence of such a place. Mother undertook all that she
thought necessary for me, and was very liberal-minded about
it. There was no nonsense about a time-table, but a good
morning's work was carried out. Breakfast over, my father
seen off to the City and the boys to school, mother would 'go
round the house'. This ritual involved such duties as putting
out sheets, counting the wash, ordering the dinner, arranging
which of the tradesmen was to be blamed for something.

Then mother would summon me to her side and open an
enormous Bible. It was invariably at the Old Testament, and
I had to read aloud the strange doings of the Patriarchs. No
comments were made, religious or otherwise, my questions
were fobbed off by references to those 'old times' or to 'bad
translations', and occasionally mother's pencil, with which she
guided me to the words, would travel rapidly over several
verses, and I heard a muttered 'never mind about that'.

After the reading, every word of one verse had to be parsed.
Very soon I learnt the queer power of the preposition, for in
such a phrase as 'the word of the Lord' I was never allowed to
say that 'Lord' was in the objective, because it involved adding that it was governed by the preposition 'of', and it was
irreverent to say that the Lord was governed by anything at
all. At the same time I knew that He *was* in the objective, and
that 'of' had done it.

After this effort mother usually gave herself up to her hobby of water-colour painting, seated at the end of the dining-room table, while I carried on by myself with a little reading, sewing, writing, or learning by heart, in the offing. Every now and again I would come to the surface with a question about the meaning of a word, or a bit of hemming that needed pressing down, or a piece of French poetry to be 'heard'. As for English poetry, it needed no hearing, because I declaimed it about the house, but the French had to be rendered carefully, with poise and a touch of éclat. I can still repeat 'Le rat de ville et le rat des champs' from the drilling of those early days.

My English history was derived from a little book in small print that dealt with the characters of the kings at some length. I learnt how one was ruthless alike to friend and foe, and how another was so weak that the sceptre fell from his nerveless grasp. I seemed to see it falling. The book had no doubts or evidence or sources, but gave all the proper anecdotes about cakes, the peaches and new ale, never smiling again, the turbulent priest, and the lighted candle. I am glad that I had these at the credulous stage, and in this unhesitating form. They were much more glowing than if they had been introduced by the chilling words 'it is said that'. I never read beyond Queen Elizabeth, and was really shocked when mother told me one day that a king had his head cut off. I rained questions on her: Who did it? Why? What had he done? Why did they let them do it?

Not as a lesson, but for sheer pleasure, did I browse in *A Child's History of Rome*, a book full of good stories that spared none of the details about Regulus in the barrel, the death of Gracchus, Marius in the pond, and Sulla's cold-blooded slaughters.

The home boasted an enormous atlas almost as big as the hearthrug, that I could only cope with when it was laid out on the floor. From this I culled a good deal, but all I can recall of my little geography book is the opening sentence, 'The Earth is an oblate spheroid', and the statement that there are seven, or five, oceans. I never could remember which, but knew it was an odd number.

For scientific notions I had Dr. Brewer's *Guide to Science*, in the form of a catechism. The author was a Trinity Hall-man, who must have made a wide appeal, for my copy (dated 1869) is of the twenty-sixth edition. It opens firmly thus: '*Q*. What is heat?', and the *A*. comes pat: 'That which produces the sensation of warmth.' Later on, however, a modern note of doubt creeps in, for we get: 'What is light?' to which the *A*. is 'The *unknown* cause of visibility'. But the field of ignorance is very small. Some of the information is human and kindly. Thus we have: '*Q*. What should a fearful person do to be secure in a storm? *A*. Draw his bedstead into the middle of his room, commit himself to the care of God, and go to bed.' To this is added, in very small print, 'No great danger needs really to be apprehended.'

I spoke of sewing, but I never progressed beyond hemming. Endless pocket-handkerchiefs for the boys were cut from the parent roll of linen, turned down at the edges by mother, and hemmed by my hot little hands while the linen was all stiff and shiny. Charles said that I put the needle in one day and took it out the next. But that was an exaggeration.

My dislike of sewing was as nothing compared to my hatred of sums. This was the correct word, for I never did anything but addition. Mother's arithmetic was at the level of the White Queen's, and I believe she was never quite sound about borrowing and paying back, especially if there were a nought or two in the top row. I had a slate on which mother put long lists of figures to be added, enough to keep me quiet for a good long time. But as the sum had been made out of her head she had to check it by working it herself. Next to ready-made pocket-handkerchiefs I think the greatest boon of modern invention would have seemed to her an arithmetic book of easy sums with answers. We certainly possessed a badly printed, delapidated old Colenso's *Arithmetic*. But this was vaguely connected in mother's mind with some one who doubted the creation of the world, and not reliable, or at least not to be encouraged. Often when sums were adumbrated I felt a little headachy, and thought I could manage a little drawing and painting instead.

Obviously there was no hard-and-fast routine in my morning's work, and if the weather turned out tempting, mother would dismiss all idea of lessons and take me out, either for a long walk, or into the West End for some shopping, or by train to Hampstead for a sketching expedition. Such times were the best part of my education, for mother had had a richly varied and adventurous life. The darker parts of it I never knew till long afterwards, but her outlook on life, her opinions on people, and her matured wisdom became a part of me. On our long tramps together, in the intervals of my bowling my hoop, I would induce her to tell me stories. She had to rake her memory for tales from Shakespeare, Jane Austen, Scott, or any novel she had ever read. But what I liked best, and insisted on hearing again and again, was a description of her own doings when she was a girl. Her first school had been at Falmouth, and after that she had gone to a 'finishing' school at Bath.

This was in the reign of William IV, when Bath was the most fashionable pleasure resort of the day. The numbers in the school were limited to six, with as many teachers as pupils. Visiting masters attended for French, music, and philosophy. Mother was frequently given lessons alone. Manners were attended to with special care. When the young ladies were invited out to tea they were set down to a meal of thick bread and butter before starting, in order that their appetites should appear elegant. They were commanded to leave something on their plate, however pleasing the dish. Nevertheless the work in school must have been solid, for mother could speak French fluently, had done a good deal of Latin, had staggered through Locke and Berkeley, and knew as much as could be expected about the movements of the moon and where to look for the various stars as the year went on.

By the way, mother started me in Latin at a very tender age. I can remember dancing round a small table chanting ' 'mo, 'mas, 'mat, 'mamus, 'matis, 'mant'. My enthusiasm was rather dashed when Tom suggested that I ought to begin the Passive Voice. This seemed to me an unnecessary complication—soldiers could so easily *go* on to the wall, without being *sent* there.

In addition to mother's stories of her school-days she used to describe her amusements in her Cornish home. She was a fine horsewoman, and had tales of giving the men 'a lead' over a high gate in the hunting-field. Balls were rare events, but they were full of go, and evidently not the stately and prim affairs of mid-Victorian times. The day following a ball was the best fun, for it was the practice of all the young men to go round on horseback and call on the girls, to 'ask how they were', and so on. Mother used to smile to herself as she dwelt on this pleasant habit.

Very few girls of her time had travelled as much as mother. Hardly had she left school before she accompanied her father abroad on his mine-prospecting journeys. The most adventurous of these was a tour in Spain. Here the so-called roads were so bad that horseback was the only means of getting about. Mother was frequently in the saddle from early morning till sundown. I thought this was lovely, but she pointed out that one could have enough even of riding. Inns were of the most primitive. One large sleeping-apartment often had to do duty for all the guests. Early one morning, after a night of this kind, the innkeeper tiptoed softly into the room and besought them in whispers to leave quietly and as soon as possible. He told them that a number of *banditti* had got wind of there being rich English people in the place, and were intending to have their money or their lives. He had given them plenty of drink which they were now sleeping off, lying about the door. In a trice mother was ready to start, for of course she had never undressed. True enough, there lay some fifteen of the fiercest-looking ruffians, each with a gleaming knife by his side, but fortunately all snoring. They had purposely disposed themselves so that no one could pass through the outer 'living-room' without treading on them. Mother gathered up her riding-skirt and stepped widely and swiftly, choosing when she could a spot near a knife, so that she could seize it if the man stirred. Rushing to the stable she saddled her horse—a job to which she was well accustomed—and rode off, knowing that her father would manage better with her out of the way.

He soon overtook her, having waited only to repay the sensible innkeeper.

An experience in Christiania was of a different and absurd nature. A visitor in the hotel was a famous chess-player, and was complaining in the lounge that he found it so difficult to get a good game—any one who would stand up to him. Whereupon it was suggested to him that mother could play very well and would keep him busy. At this mother was horrified, but instead of singing low she merely declined rather haughtily, for she thought the man odiously conceited. However, he so begged and implored, and mother's friends so egged her on with 'Do beat him, Mary', in undertones, that she said, 'Very well, then, I will give you just one game, but no more.' Overjoyed, he hurried out the pieces, they sat down, and the friends watched eagerly. Mother fool's-mated him. It was one of those moments that make life worth living. She rose, bowed, and retired from the scene, leaving him a lather of excuses and annoyance—a humbler man.

Such reminiscences were for country walks. A visit to the West End was a different affair. My delight was to walk down Regent Street and gaze in the shop-windows, pointing out all the things I would like to have. And this was as good a piece of education as any other, for I early acquired the Londoner's ability to enjoy things without buying them. For even in our palmiest days mother never dreamt of buying anything she didn't really want. But how we both gazed at and admired exotic fruits, exquisite note-paper, china jugs (a weakness of mother's), and especially drawing-materials with serried rows of paints. One day in Bond Street mother noticed a sailor hat, poised alone in a window. 'How nice and simple! the very thing for you!' she exclaimed, and went in to ask the price. 'Three guineas, Madam.' She nearly fell out of the shop.

A picture gallery was often a reason for our going into the West End. The Turner room at the National was as familiar to me as the dining-room at home, and mother early taught me to regard these pictures as my own property. 'Given to the nation,' she would roll on her tongue as she feasted her eyes on the *Fighting Téméraire*. Then there were the Dudley and the Grosvenor galleries, wherein enthusiasts were few. Around the solemnly quiet rooms I would march with a catalogue, ticking those I liked, and condemning those that seemed feeble.

On one of these visits to the Grosvenor I spied a white kitten belonging to the cloakroom attendant. Noting my fervour, she offered to give it to me. Mother had no heart to refuse, and home it was taken, in a skewered fish-basket provided by the attendant. That journey home in the bus! The kitten wobbled about, pushing its nose almost through every weak spot in the basket. At every frantic mew there were pained looks from humane passengers, and mutters of 'Crool'. 'What shall we call it, mother?' 'Sir Coutts Lindsey,' was the reply, because he had founded or presided over the Gallery. So Coutty was established with milk and buttered feet, and ruled the mice and us for several years. She must have been a tom, for she never produced any kittens, much to my disappointment.

Taking long walks in the country was the main relaxation in those days when even bicycles, or velocipedes as they were called, were rare enough to be stared at. My father's plan for a half-holiday when no cricket was to be had was usually to go with all the boys to Barnet or Potters Bar by train, and then walk far afield, twenty miles or more, returning dog-tired to a huge supper. Perhaps I was a bit envious of these outings. Whatever the reason, on one memorable day my father borrowed me, all alone, to go for a country walk with him. We started from Hampstead Heath Station as a base, and seemed to go a tremendous distance along lanes and across fields. I seized the chance to ask my father about his school-days. He could remember only two things about his boarding-school: one was that he had a barrel of apples sent him on a birthday, so heavy that it took two men to bring it in. The other memory was that he wrote home when he was twelve to say that he now knew quite enough, and might as well leave school. He laughed, but it seemed to me reasonable enough, for twelve was a big age, and he certainly knew everything. I believed all

he said, and readily imagined that Gog and Magog came down
to dinner every day in Guildhall when they heard the clock
strike one, and even to this day I feel that guinea-pigs' eyes are
not firmly set in their heads.

On this walk we grew very hungry, and then came the top
of my pride and happiness, for we went into a little wayside
inn with a sanded floor and sat in a parlour with coloured
pictures and the sun coming in through a tiny window. Bread
and cheese and beer were ordered! Well, if that wasn't being
grown up and like the boys, what was? Beer tasted horrible
to me as a rule, but this seemed ambrosial.

Barring such occasional jaunts to town or country, my morn-
ings were 'busy', while mother was light-heartedly painting.
She said to me one day, 'Molly dear, I feel that I ought to be
worrying.' 'What about, mother?' 'Oh, nothing in particular,
just worrying.'

The afternoons were my own, and I generally spent them
in my own room. Here I was complete monarch. There was
no attempt in those days to furnish a room to suit the occupant,
and most of mine was taken up by a huge wooden bed and a
huge chest of drawers. However, it had a jolly window looking down the street. As it was directly under the study, there
was a chance for a postal system from one window to the other.
A basket on a string would be let down by one of the boys
and dangled in front of me. Pulling it in I would find a letter,
asking me to fetch him a pair of scissors or a particular book.
This I would find and place in the basket to be hauled up.
Letters too of sheer camaraderie were passed to and fro, written on small fancy note-paper and envelopes. Several of these
I still possess. The burden of most of them is a hope that I am
quite well, but one begs me to take more than eighteenpence
when I go to buy his (Barnholt's) birthday present, as 'there
are some very fine stamp-albums to be got in the Upper Street
for half-a-crown'.

As I lay awake in the morning I could see the houses opposite and a good bit of the street. I liked to hear the 'milk' cry
of the women who carried the pails on yokes, and the cheery

rat-tat of the postman, but the sweep's long-drawn wail used to fill me with misery when he made his rare rounds. One morning as I lay idly watching the house opposite I had one of the surprises of my life. A broom suddenly shot out of a chimney. I never thought of connecting this fairy-tale event with the sweep, and thought mother's explanation very dull. I ought to have asked my father.

Before I fell asleep at night I watched a room in the house opposite. All was rather vague until they lit up, and then there was glory. They were real people who walked about and talked and did things just like ourselves. But hardly had things begun to hum when some one would go and draw the curtains. This seemed heartless. Although mother had curtains (for respectability, I suppose), she never drew them. 'If people like to look in,' she would say to visitors who remarked on the fact, 'they are quite welcome. I am not engaged in murder or coining, or anything that calls for reserve.'

Long afternoons I spent in my room alone, while the boys were at school. Drawing and painting took most of the time, but there was also the curious occupation of cutting patterns in perforated cardboard, sticking them on a piece of coloured ribbon, and inflicting them on some aunts as a Bible bookmark. I had a boyish contempt for dolls, especially the flaxen-haired blue-eyed type, whose clothes wouldn't take off. These came in handy as an audience, for one of my favourite games was to hang over the foot of my bed, and preach to the counterpane, with a text duly given out twice, in different directions.

I must have done this to break the silence. No London child to-day can realize the quiet of the road on which my window looked. A tradesman's cart, a hawker or a hurdy-gurdy, were the sum total of the usual traffic. Sometimes everything had been so quiet for so long that the sound of a passer-by or of a butcher's pony would take on a distant, unreal tone, as if it were mocking me. This frightened me, and I would break the spell by singing 'The Lass of Richmond Hill'.

Music I made for myself with broken nibs stuck into the edge of my table. The tinkle was cheering, but no tune could

I achieve, although Charles made effective ones on his 'organ' of nibs.

In spite of my contempt for dolls of the usual kind, and my intense hatred of sewing, I took great delight in dressing up the pawns of a very large set of chess-men, discarded by the family. White pawns became Arthur's knights or Greek heroes, as the fancy took me, black ones were pagans or Trojans. Bright bits of velvet and silk were sewn on them by my toiling fingers, and cardboard swords fitted to their sides. The best bits of stuff and passionate care were expended on Sir Lancelot, who slaughtered pagans with easy grace on my washing-stand.

Speaking of the washing-stand reminds me that I made a kind of sundial on it, being, however, quite ignorant of the existence of such a thing. Noticing that the afternoon sun kept shifting all the time from soap-dish to basin, from basin to tooth-glass, I conceived the idea of using it as a clock. Pencil marks were made on the marble top, and 3 o'clock, quarter past three, half-past three, and so on were neatly written beside them. Having no confidence, however, in the sun's behaviour, I would run to the top of the stairs and call out to one of the servants to tell me the time. 'By the right, or by the dining-room, Miss?' 'By the right, please.' And if it came anywhere near agreeing with my clock, Galileo himself can hardly have had a greater thrill.

A feast for the Arthurian Round Table was sometimes planned. The lid of a bonnet-box was placed on the floor, and the pawns arranged round. I would slip into the kitchen when pastry was being made, beg for a little lump, shape it into tiny tarts, twelve, put jam on them, and smuggle them into the oven. When cook declared them done, they were taken upstairs and laid out on dolls' plates. On one such occasion my pride induced me to invite Barnholt to 'come and see' when he came home from school. He could be trusted not to laugh at my banquet. Looking grave and impressed with its grandeur, he proceeded to pop all the tarts into his mouth, because they were too much for the tiny insides of the pawns. 'I have saved all their lives,' said he, with such solemnity that I was truly grateful to him.

Of course I had a shelf for my books. We were none of us too fond of showing our books to visitors. They didn't really care about them and sometimes would wet their fingers to turn over the pages. My own treasures are nearly all with me still, showing only the honourable marks of age and continual reading—no thumb-marks, no dogs' ears, no loose leaves. *Rosy's Voyage Round the World* was prime favourite. A little girl and three boys go out in a rowing-boat, sight Africa, find Crusoe's island, catch an eel, light a fire to cook it . . . and so on, in such a realistic way that I was as convinced of the extent of their travels as they were themselves. Each adventure had a full-page illustration by Lorenz Frolich. *The Little Gipsy*, also illustrated by him, was the story of an only child who is stolen by gipsies because of her lovely voice, brought up by them, and after terrible adventures becomes a famous singer and finds her parents. *Alice in Wonderland* we all knew practically by heart, and one of the red-letter days of my life was a birthday when I received from my father *Through the Looking-glass*. I got through the morning somehow, and then buried myself in it all the afternoon, my pleasure enhanced by the knowledge that there was a boring visitor downstairs to whom I ought to be making myself agreeable. And it was about chess-men! As I handle the book now I live over again that enchanted afternoon.

The pictures in our books were well drawn, but colour was very rare and highly prized. Just before the Christmas of 1872, mother took me to Oxford Street to do some shopping. Our main object was to buy a birthday present for Charles. I can remember mounting the stairs at Bumpus's amid what seemed to me thousands of books—a land of Canaan indeed. The stairs are still there, and I prefer them to the lift, because they recall that golden day. Mother chose *The Story without an End*. The story itself was an allegory, and was too subtle for us, but it is impossible to describe the endless pleasure given us all by those full-page pictures, whose colours are as fresh and beautiful to-day as when Charles received them 'on his tenth birthday', as the inscription in mother's hand-writing records.

It was entirely due to its colour that another book became my constant companion. This was an illustrated Scripture text-book, given to me on my seventh birthday, and still preserved. I have never come across another like it. Some of the little pictures are very crude, but most of them, especially such short commands as 'Walk Honestly', 'Fear God', in fancy lettering, with gold and bright-coloured borders, are tasteful enough.

Some of the boys' prizes fell into my keeping, handed to me in disgust. One of these, *The Safe Compass*, afforded me many a joyful hour. It took the gloomiest views as to the fate of the disobedient. But if you left out everything that was in italics, and altered the endings of the plots, the stories were good. The disobedient were gored by bulls, those who laughed at the infirm fell down wells and were crippled for life, busy mockers died in want . . . there was no lack of gripping incident. But sometimes one could improve on the plot. For instance, Joe had a beautiful toy boat. Fritz (ominous name) was jealous and destroyed it privily. Joe planned revenge. Knowing that Fritz passed by every day with a basket of eggs, Joe tied a piece of string across the road, hid in the hedge, and waited for the crash. Traffic along the lane was obviously not congested, but who should happen along in front of Fritz but the good Herbert. Joe called to him to come into the hedge too, and enjoy the disaster. Instead of entering into the spirit of the thing, Herbert went into italics about coals of fire, the string was hauled in, and when Fritz appeared he was kindly invited to tea. Now conversion was all right and proper, but surely it might have come *after* the egg-smash?

Many people of my age must have imbibed their early religious notions from the same book that I did—*The Peep of Day*, for my copy is dated 1872, and is one of the three hundred and forty-seventh thousand. It is very insistent and realistic about hell, and apparently there is only one virtue, obedience to parents and kind teachers, which leads of itself to a life of bliss 'beyond the sky'. One stanza of verse attracted me greatly:

> *Satan is glad—when I am bad,*
> *And hopes that I—with him shall lie*
> *In fire and chains—and dreadful pains.*

Whether the rhythm pleased me, or whether I was gratified that such an important person as Satan would actually welcome my company, I can't say, but the idea was more exciting than that of heaven put forth by the author. The stories about Jesus I liked best, and admired Him greatly. What a pity, I thought, that after such a good life He should have told an untruth at the last. This is what I read: 'Jesus just tasted the vinegar, and said, "It is finished."' My idea was that he had been given this horrid stuff to drink, tasted it, and then out of politeness pretended that he had finished it up.

I suppose that like all children I never asked any one about the things that really puzzled me, although I was ready enough to ask questions for the sake of asking. When obliged to sit and be polite listening to a visitor's conversation, I used to break the monotony with an innocent question, always prefaced by the phrase 'What means by?' Thus I would ask, 'What means by poison?' 'What means by lottery?' 'What means by jealous?' Mother would enter into explanations, only too thankful, I fancy, to find something to talk about. But one day she turned upon me, thoroughly exasperated, because I had asked, 'What means by Russia?' It seemed to me quite a promising opening, and I never knew why it suddenly enraged her.

Alone, in my room, I pondered over much. Once I was perturbed more seriously than a grown-up ever imagines. God had very kindly made the world, but suppose the notion had never occurred to Him? Suppose there had never been any God? Suppose there had never been anything at all? I was so devastated by the thought that I had to run about violently up and down stairs to kill the demon.

VI

School-days

WHILE my brothers were quite small they went to a
private school close by, kept by a very tall, thin,
severe old Scot, whose notion of the evil in the world
was summed up in 'smoking and drinking and going to theay-
ters'. A sound knowledge of grammar seemed to be the chief
end of man. Tom was the first to enjoy the excitement of
'going to school'. He came home one day full of the news
that there was to be an examination on the morrow.

'Mother, what is an examination?'

'Oh, nothing much, dear. They want to see what you know,
and you write it down.'

Alas for definitions, poor little Tom must have spent the
intervening time in anxious thought. No sooner was the class
provided with paper and pen than he began to write down all
he knew. He had got no farther than 'I know that the earth
goes round the sun' when the real nature of the business was
explained.

After a while the school grew too big for the house, and a
room was hired in Canonbury Tower for some of the classes.
The boys enjoyed the change of walking through the few
yards of street and racing up into the old building. The window overhangs the street in Tudor fashion, and it was here
that Barnholt liked to sit. He used to fasten a stone to a piece of
string, and let it down on to the hat of a passer-by. If he could
pull it up before the bewildered man had discovered him,
he scored a point in a game with another boy similarly armed.

What was taught at this school no one quite knew, but
every one brought home a prize at the end of the year, even
Barnholt, 'for the general work of the class', and when the
time came for entering a public school the boys did well
enough. Shrewsbury was chosen for Tom, merely, I think,

because it was on the Welsh border and near my father's old home. It was a long journey in those days, and seeing Tom off for the 'half-year' made quite a little stir in the family, while welcoming him home was a grand occasion, calling for a feast, and my 'sitting up'. Things were to be done and seen 'when Tom comes home'. For one of these home-comings I had prepared for weeks by saving up all the pennies that came my way, and hiding them in my bottom drawer, till there was a fair copper mine there. On the day after his return I took Tom solemnly into my room and unveiled the treasure, with the words, 'For you.' To my disappointment he refused to take them—a lesson to me through life never to refuse a gift.

What Tom learnt at Shrewsbury was clear enough—Latin and Greek, with the ancient history and geography pertaining to them. The only English literature that reached him were lines to be put into Latin verse, while Milton was used for punishment. There is a pencil note in his copy of *Paradise Lost*: 'Had to write 500 lines of this for being caught reading *King Lear* in class.' The only modern geography that he knew was the map of Scotland, because this too was chosen as a punishment. Once he tried to avoid having to copy it again by rubbing out the 'T. W.' at the bottom—the initials of the master, 'old Thos. Webster'. But T. W. was too sharp for him. 'Very nice,' said he, 'my dear Thomas, but you neglected to rub out my private mark under the Isle of Rum.' He experienced a flogging, kneeling on the big Bible in the school hall. Once he was within an ace of being expelled for making a snow-storm in a preposter's room by dropping showers of paper through a hole in the ceiling. Moss, the head master, summoned Tom to the dread 'study', and was looking up a train for his immediate departure, when a noble schoolfellow knocked at the door and produced some kind of alibi for Tom. No doubt Moss, not long appointed and hardly more than a boy himself, was glad of any excuse to avoid an expulsion, and no more was done. Gilkes was the only master Tom revered.

Not encouraged by Tom's career, my father chose a day-school for the other three boys, and obtained presentations to Merchant Taylors'. The entrance examination was no great ordeal. Indeed, there was a legend that you needed only to be able to spell 'separate' and 'parliament', and to know who Jeroboam was. These bits of information were drilled into Barnholt's head when his turn came, and all was well.

At the family tea at five o'clock we heard various bits of school gossip, and the names of the masters were printed on my memory. 'Jala', the short for J. A. L. Airey, the mathematics master, was naturally Dym's chief god. Charles was extraordinarily lucky in having a real artist for his drawing-master, Mr. Fahey, who found in him a pupil after his own heart and managed to shield Charles from the demands of other subjects. Mr. Bamfield, affectionately called 'Bammy', was the classics master and Henri Bué the French master, with Mr. Storr later on.

Although Charles successfully avoided doing anything much beside drawing he never got into trouble. Never observed to laugh himself, he would be the cause of laughter in others, doing some trick and preserving a face of disapproving innocence. Many's the time at home that Barnholt was sent out of the room for unseemly bursts of laughter when it was Charles who had set him off. Once, however, at school Charles was caught red-handed throwing stones impiously at the figure of Sir Thomas White. He defended himself by the curious plea that this was the only thing against which there was no rule. The master, a bit nonplussed, had no ready reply, and while he thought it over Charles faded away.

He came home in high delight one evening, having shone beyond all the others in the French lesson. Some three or four times during the reading of the French play Mr. Storr was reminded of a parallel passage in Horace. Before he could quote it, 'Ah yes, Sir,' chipped in Charles, 'does it not go something like this?'—and neatly, but with becoming hesitation spouted the Latin line. Mr. Storr was delighted, and when this happened twice more, enthusiastic. 'I am very pleased, my boy, that you have such a feeling for literature.' He did not know that Charles was using Tom's copy of the play. Tom had also been reminded of Horace, and had written the appropriate quotations at the side.

No master seemed to have taught Barnholt anything, and all he brought home was detention-cards. 'Never mind,' mother used to say, 'mark my words, he will be the first to earn his own living.' And she was right.

So much did I hear about the school and the masters that I feel almost an old Taylorian myself (especially since I have had two sons there). On one day every year I seemed to get right inside the life of the boys. The Feast of St. Barnabas has been Speech Day at the school from time immemorial. The weather was always fine, and I was fixed into a pretty summer frock and taken by mother to Charterhouse Square. Here in the great Hall I felt, for a time at least, superior to the boys. For I was ushered to a proper seat, and given a printed programme, while they were all huddled at the back, by the great fireplace. The plays and speeches in French and Latin and Greek and Hebrew gave me plenty of unintelligent excitement. There were definite points for which I could watch. Dym told us that the Members of the Company were provided with a copy of the speeches, with hints where to laugh at the jokes, so that the parents should realize how well they knew their classics. When they laughed, therefore, I knew. Another diversion was to count the number of times that the Head Master, Dr. Baker, would call out 'Sit down, every boy.' Charles had so often imitated the nervous agitation with which these words were uttered that it would have been dull indeed if 'every boy' had been obedient. The next excitement was to see Dym walk up for a prize, always a certainty. One year Charles actually had a prize for Latin—a quite unreadable book, magnificently bound. It stood on our shelves as a monument of what Charles could achieve by sheer humbug. But he always had the head prize for drawing, which once was a colossal paint-box, stocked with all sorts of new shades of colours, probably ordered for him by Mr. Fahey.

Another treat to me was the school song ('Homo plantat'), which I knew so well that I was able to join in, and dazzle the fat mothers around me by my familiarity with the Latin words. But all feelings of superiority were bowled over by the procession of the Master and Wardens, or whatever they were, of the Merchant Taylors Company, in their robes and chains, with their fur collars and bouquets. The chief one, who had been enthroned, and saluted by each prize-taking boy, looked to me exactly like the Lord God mentioned so often in Genesis.

After the solemnities the fun. To be allowed to see a real classroom, where boys behaved badly, with desks all inky and carved with names, a desk where the master sat, and a notice-board; to run out on the great green, where the masters were swishing about in gowns and hoods, being agreeable to mothers, and where the grand senior boys were still walking about in the stage clothes in which they had been acting—all this was a kind of awful delight.

It is hardly surprising that I cast longing thoughts on going to school myself. So in my twelfth year mother decided to send me to an 'Establishment for Young Ladies' about a mile from home. It must have been to give me some companion-ship, for I can conceive no other rational motive for the step. Indeed, I have come to think that the main value of school life is to prevent one's getting on too fast in the natural surround ings of home.

My first day is photographed in my memory. Of course I was delirious with excitement, and sped along Highbury New Park as though on air. I was placed in the lowest class with three other little girls of my own age, who were reading aloud the story of Richard Arkwright. I say 'reading', but unless I had had a book I should have understood not a word of their jerky mumblings. Meanwhile I got interested in this barber who outdid his rivals by shaving people for a half-penny, and when my turn came to read I held forth delightedly. Soon there was a whispered consultation with the Authorities, and I was removed then and there into a higher class. Here were three or four big girls. They seemed to me so big as almost to be of the 'aunt' type. But my fear of them soon disappeared, for the sounds coming from them purporting to be French were even worse than the English reading had been. Again I sailed ahead, and was asked by the teacher if I had been to France. 'No,' said I, 'but my mother has a lot.' (I need hardly say that I soon found it best to fall in with the pronunciation used by the others, much to poor mother's chagrin.)

At lunch-time I was questioned by the girls as to my full name, what my father was, how many brothers I had, and how big a house. After this came instructions for the next day and the acquisition of lovely new exercise-books and a new history book, and then I fled triumphantly home, to find mother waiting for me with the front door open. She embraced me as though I had come from Australia or some great peril, breathed the word 'darling', and no more.

My sense of triumph and complacency was short-lived, for the next day, as you may guess, there was an arithmetic lesson. Absurd as it may seem, it is the cold truth that I had done plenty of shopping and had managed the change, and yet in my twelfth year I had never seen an £ *s. d.* sum laid out, and had to be told what the symbols stood for. Hill Difficulty was nothing to the task of turning farthings into pence, pence into shillings, and shillings into pounds. Then I was expected to take a halfpenny from a farthing, which seemed the height of absurdity. The other girls went to work with easy assurance, raising the eyebrow a little at my dismay. Worse was in store, for there followed something they called 'mental arithmetic', of which I had never heard. The mistress stood up and gave forth sums from her head, and, without any slate to work them out on, the girls shouted the answers. One kind of sum smacked to me of black magic: 'Twelve articles at fourpence three farthings each, how much altogether?' Hardly were the words out of the teacher's mouth before the answer came. A kind girl next me told me in a hurried whisper to keep the pence and turn the farthings into threepences. But why? And what were the 'articles' that one could buy so quickly? And supposing you only wanted ten?

However, I soon learnt not to ask for explanations, for the explanations were far worse than the original difficulty. For instance, we had object lessons, one day on a snail, another day on a candle, each time a pleasant surprise. The teacher read them out of a little book. 'How a pin is made' greatly attracted me. I had used pins without ever thinking, and now I suddenly saw that it must need quite an effort to make one. So I attended carefully. Still there were gaps in my grasp of the process, and I went to the mistress in our lunch-interval, and begged her to explain it to me. 'Oh, yes, dear,' said she, and opening her book read aloud to me very slowly and emphatically just what she had said before. 'You see now, don't you, dear?' 'Oh, yes, I see now, thank you,' said I brightly, lest she should read it again.

Similar assertions of perfect understanding were ready after an explanation of the treatment of remainders in short division. Short! Surely the word was used in sarcasm. I always 'did it by long'. No one bothered about method or understanding or anything as long as you got the answer. A kind of sum that gave me immense trouble was this: 'A man has £85 13s. 4½d. To how many children can he give £7 16s. 1¾d.?' Well, I proceeded to dole it out, subtracting and subtracting, until my paper ran short. Even when, after an hour's work, the man was reduced to practically nothing more, I never could be sure of the number of his beneficiaries ticked off on the many bits of paper. One evening at home Dym caught me at this task, and began to laugh.

'Good Lord!' he exclaimed. 'Don't they teach you how to . . . Look here, darling, can you do simple long division?'

'Oh, yes, Dym,' said I hopefully, for that was my long suit.

He breathed something about fractions, but seeing my blank face, showed me how to bring everything to farthings, and then see how many times I could take the little heap from the big heap—by division.

'And will the answer be in children?' said I; 'because it's got to be.'

'Of course,' said he. And when I got to school it was right. This incident was a Rosetta Stone, for I at last understood why one had had to do reduction, which had seemed to me a silly waste of time.

Not that time mattered. In school 'time was all withdrawn'. This was brought home to me by a curious experience one dreary morning. I was seated with my school-fellows at a long table, copying again and again 'Alfred Tennyson is a poet', my writing getting steadily worse as the hated statement was repeated. Doubt began—perhaps people had denied that he was a poet? Glancing up at the school clock to see how far off it still was to the lunch-interval at a quarter to eleven, I beheld a miracle. As I looked, the big hand slipped from ten past ten to twenty past! If the sun had done a similar turn in the sky I could not have been more astonished. And it was not an answer to a prayer like Joshua's, though it might well have been. I watched to see what would happen next: the clock resumed its usual duty at twenty past, and nobody noticed anything. We had lunch-time by the clock, and I was too glad of this to point out what I had seen. But thenceforward all clocks for me lost something of their authority. At home we all 'went' by the dining-room clock, which was regularly kept at ten minutes fast, 'to be on the safe side', as mother said. She also confided to me once that it caused visitors to go a little earlier than they otherwise might to catch a train, for she had observed that they never trusted their own watches. I can hear her saying, 'Our clock is most reliable,' which of course was perfectly true.

I have no recollection of any time-table at school, and I rather think that the authorities yielded to clamour oftener than we suspected. But it was usual to do a little Scripture every morning. This consisted in writing out and reciting a verse or two, fortunately without religious comment. One day we were told as a great treat that we might for the following day learn *any* text we like, and recite it as a little surprise.

'I know which I shall choose,' I whispered to my neighbour. Alas! I had been overheard by the lady at the head of the table.

'I fear, Mary dear, that you are being irreverent. I know which text you mean—a very short one.'

I felt disgraced, but when I came to think of it, how did she guess which one I meant if she hadn't been a bit irreverent herself?

My new history book was *Little Arthur*, which one could read like a delightful story. The general spirit of the author about unpleasant things seemed to be that they happened so long ago that they probably never happened at all. Anyhow, we gained a fair idea of the flow of events and the stories of leading people without boredom. Alongside of this we were drilled in the dates of the kings and queens, and could say them off like the multiplication table, for which I have ever been grateful.

What demon invented 'freehand copies'? And why this name? Anything less free it would be hard to imagine. While Charles was being encouraged to plunge away and paint at Merchant Taylors', we poor girls used to waste the precious hours labelled 'Drawing' in slavishly copying the design of a vase, or a fancy scroll, printed on a card. The only trouble was to get both sides exactly alike. It was 'corrected', rubbed out, improved, and finally 'clear-lined', that is firmly and fiercely drawn over with a freshly sharpened pencil. It might take two hours to complete one of these horrors; then you turned a new page and were given another. Nothing else was done until you got to the top class, where the big girls copied shaded cottages.

By far the best part of those school-days was the play-time, for the other girls were a jolly lot, whose names and faces and peculiarities I remember as though it were yesterday. Our liberal lunch-intervals were spent in games of tip-and-run and rounders in the big garden, from which we came in all hot and panting. And we hatched schemes of small wickednesses, in which I was always made to take the lead, 'because you always look so innocent, Mary, she'll never guess it's you'.

Indeed I could usually put up some plausible talk and keep my countenance, but sometimes my power of self-control was strained. The lady of the object lessons taught us English from a book called *Butter's Spelling*. There were lists of words derived from Latin, with the Latin word at the top. When she pronounced *miles* as if it were a measure of length, I thought it was some curious conceit of her own, but when in the poetry lesson she spoke of Horatius Cocles as if he were a shell-fish, I exploded into a sudden burst of laughter. 'What do you see that is funny, little Mary?' I blushed and stammered out that the pattern of the wall-paper had suddenly struck me as funny. She looked at it and at me in a puzzled way, but the matter blew over, and no one was any the wiser. Except of course the boys at tea-time, who loved to hear the strange revelations of a girls' school.

Of bosom friends I had none at all, but kept several of my school-fellows in fee. The walk home was long and boring, so I would induce any one 'coming my way' to accompany me, or more often to go out of their way to do so. I would ask them to hold my books 'just while I get my gloves on'. On the principle of the Arabian Nights those gloves were never completely buttoned, while I distracted the attention of the book-carrier with the doings of the boys or with stories about the siege of Troy. My victim would sometimes protest, but generally ended by carrying my books almost to my door, and agitated next day for a similar job if I would go on with the story. For some curious reason my memory always failed me if my arms were cumbered up with books.

One big girl, in a long skirt and with her hair done up, hated me. I had once openly set her right on a horrible pronunciation of a French word, and thenceforth she snubbed me whenever she could. One day I could bear this no longer, and with all my force let fly a blow at her most accessible spot, which annoyed me by its mere size. Holding herself as though in great pain she went straight to the head mistress and lodged a complaint. This turn of events was quite new to me —telling! Whatever would happen next? I was summoned to the drawing-room and told that such a blow might be very serious, might set up a terrible internal disease and cause perchance *death*. Never shall I forget that afternoon and evening. Suppose Louisa Roberts were to die? For me then the gallows. Disgrace and a harrowing end faced me. I had to practise my music, but what was the good when I had to die so soon? I didn't dare to tell mother, lest she should begin recriminations. I looked longingly at Charles, who would make light of even the Judgement Day, but again dreaded that even he would be horrified at having a murderer for a sister. All through tea-time I could think of nothing but the gallows, and I don't know how I got through the evening and long night. As early as decently possible the next morning I rushed off to school. Racing along Highbury New Park I passed the school and made for the road towards Louisa's house, so that I might know the worst. Expecting to see something in the nature of a funeral, or straw laid down in the street, what was my astonish-ment at seeing Louisa herself, bouncing along, swinging her books by the strap, red in the face as usual! 'Hullo, Mary, good morning,' says she. 'You're rather early, aren't you?' My relief was so great that I came near giving her another blow for her heartlessness. Probably it is the memory of that dread-ful experience that has made me doubtful of the wisdom of 'reasoning' with children instead of giving them a short sharp punishment.

Private animosities were few, but there was always a sup-pressed war going on between the Scottish girls in the school and the English ones. The head mistress was Scottish herself, and had married a Scot, and of course Scottish pupils were attracted on this account. The glories of their country were thrust upon us in season and out: its scenery was unrivalled, its education marvellous, it had never really been conquered by England, it had given us our kings. . . . We English under-dogs used to hold indignation-meetings, raised to fever-pitch one day when we had been told that an Edinburgh medical degree was better than a London one. The daughter of a doc-tor lost the power of speech on this point. What a pity that we had never heard of the 'inferiority complex'—how we might have scored!

The old Scot was the typical sandy-haired, raw-boned dominie, in long frock coat and skull cap. Scottish education may have been marvellous, but his only method was to make us learn a great deal of rubbish by heart. Of course the capes and bays, and county towns, of Scotland, England, and Ireland, but we also committed to memory not only the provinces of France, but also the departments, with their chief towns (quite apart from the map). Beautiful maps we certainly drew, all blue round the edges, and decorated with imaginary rivers, which frequently flowed through the mountain-ranges. Scotland was the usual subject of these, varied by the Holy Land, where I thought the rivers were actually of milk and honey.

However, our geography lessons were our greatest treat. So popular did they become, and our clamour for them so intense, that the foolish old man would allow them to absorb a great part of the day. As soon as we had been 'heard' a few facts out of the book the game began—a game as devoid of skill as any I have played. We sat in a semicircle round the desk. The master would then announce the name of some obscure town in the British Isles, known only to its intimates and Bradshaw. Each of us then in turn made a guess at the county. The girl who guessed right went to the top of the class. After a score of guesses had been made the position of the town made no impression at all, but that didn't matter, the amount of bustle and fun was superb. If by good chance a Cornish town was named I was sick with suspense that some girl would guess it before my turn, and I had to preserve a poker face lest my joy should appear. For they all knew I was Cornish.

Where the old fellow came out really strong was in Grammar. It is almost incredible, but we spent a whole term on the first two scenes of *The Tempest*. As soon as we had read round once, or even without reading at all, we began to 'take places' for parsing. This was not such a wild gamble as the geography because we had to be careful. Every single word was parsed fully, and if a girl omitted the gender or person of the commonest noun, or made the slightest slip, she lost her place to the girl who detected it. It became a point of honour to go as fast as we could, and we learnt to parse like the wind, as much as possible in a breath. Thus, 'common - noun - third - person - singular - number - neuter - gender - objective - case - governed by - the - preposition - of'. It seems absurd to do this with Shakespeare, but it was better than being bored with the learned notes at the end of the play.

The old fellow never laughed, but he had a few jokes that remain with me from their frequent repetition. One referred to the conceit of a young minister of religion who was invited to take Prayers in a school. Turning to the Head, he asked what prayer would be best to say. 'We usually say the Lord's Prayer,' replied the Head, 'but of course, if you know a better one, please use it.' By experience we knew that this was the point where laughter was expected. Another joke also dealt with a young minister. He was praying 'from the bosom', and besought the Lord that his congregation might not be 'like Galileo, who cared for none of these things'.

This joke tickled mother immensely, and she tried it on a visitor, saying airily, 'You see, Mrs. Peatty, in the matter of politics I'm like Galileo. I care for none of these things.' To her dismay, Mrs. Peatty replied quite seriously, 'Oh, quite, so am I.'

'Well, mother,' said the boys, 'now you see what comes of being funny.'

VII

Sunday

THE mere word 'Sunday' is apt to give a mental shiver to people of long memories. The outer world closed down. It was wrong to travel except for dire necessity, and then very difficult. It was wrong to work, and wrong to play. In fact, existence in some houses was so dull that Tom said he understood the full meaning of the opening verse of the 122nd Psalm. However, we did the best we could with the day, and it had the advantage of my father being with us all the time. He didn't take religion *too* seriously, and left it to mother to enforce all her superstitious restrictions that she had imbibed in her Cornish home.

She for her part put all the cheerfulness she could into the food, against which there seemed to be no Biblical taboo. Instead of the daily tea for breakfast we had coffee—lashings of real strong coffee, with a great jug of hot milk. When the season allowed we always had sausages ('the British weekly'). But while these appetizing smells were around us we had to learn the Collect and get it 'heard' before breakfast. One blessed Sunday after Trinity produced a Collect so free from fulsome flattery, so quick off the mark in its demands, that we learnt it in no time. Even now a Collect smells to me of coffee.

Breakfast over, the whole family walked in detachments to St. Paul's Cathedral. We had reduced the route to a science, by side streets, short cuts by the New River, along parts of Essex Road, the City Road, Goswell Road, and Aldersgate, and finally past 'the highest point of London' in Panyer Alley to the north door of the cathedral. I must have been very little when I did this long walk, because I once described it as 'continully cwossing'. My father explained to me that the more slantingly you crossed a road the shorter it was. He also alleviated the walk by playing wayside cribbage, a favourite game in the country. In town the points for scoring had to be rather different; thus we had: man carrying baby, 5; three in a hansom, 5; perambulator, 1; cat in a window, 15; ladder, 1; man with a mourning hatband, 5; any one we knew to speak to (very rare), 31, game. I think we must have played this when mother was walking behind, or this game would never have slipped through her rules.

Sometimes mother and I went by tram, but the horse affair was so slow, the waiting for it so long, and the stoppings so frequent, that the walkers reached Aldersgate before we did. Occasionally my father would vary the route home by taking us through the deserted City, free of all traffic, and showing us Austin Friars and funny little passages, till we came to Broad Street and thence back to Canonbury by train.

How cool and vast the cathedral seemed after the dusty streets! We walked with precision to our special seats, for the vergers knew us well. My father had a stall, my brothers sat in a pew beyond the choir, my mother and I sat in the reserved front row under the dome. The cathedral seemed to belong to us, and little took place that escaped the notice of one or other of us.

My back still aches in memory of those long services. Nothing was spared us—the whole of the 'Dearly beloved', never an omission of the Litany, always the full ante-Communion Service, involving a sermon of unbelievable length. The seats and kneeling-boards were constructed for grown-ups (and not too comfortable for them), and a child had the greatest difficulty in keeping an upright kneeling position all through the long intoned Litany. We found some alleviations even here. How would the officiating priest take the fence in intoning 'uncharitableness'? Canon Milman was our delight over this, because he used to quaver forth '-table-' all by itself and leave a long pause of suspense before he could reach the high note of '-ness'. After this we looked forward to beating down Satan under our feet, partly because it seemed a nice final thing to do, and partly because it was the half-way mark. Some energetic clergymen put in extra prayers at the end, even the thanksgiving—always associated with my blackest thoughts.

Like all children I put some kind of workable meaning into the strange Prayer Book phrases. 'The Scripture moveth us in sundry places' must mean that it pokes us in various parts of our body—a spiritual dig in the ribs: 'Come now, own up.'

'Deal not with us after our sins' was surely a foolish request. Mother's indignant refusal to 'deal with' the butcher was her last word of annoyance, and why should we go out of our way to pray for such treatment? Still more idiotic did it seem to pray, 'Neither reward us after our iniquities.' If God was so generously inclined, why prevent him? As for asking him to rule the Church in the right way, that was mere impertinence. Surely he could be trusted to do it rightly!

Curiously enough I did actually seek enlightenment on two difficulties. Walking home with Barnholt I asked him what 'begotten' meant. He wasn't quite sure, but thought it was pretty much the same as 'forgotten'. I was satisfied, and never pushed any farther, concluding that to be the only one 'forgotten' was just one of those odd things that happened to Jesus. The other difficulty was a sin mentioned in the Litany as being a 'deadly' one. On this point I approached mother. In a sudden burst of confidence worthy of Micawber, she told me that she had puzzled over this herself. Enough. Why worry, when even grown-ups didn't know?

On the few occasions that they chanted the Athanasian Creed I suffered much. Not from the Creed itself, which was a change and amused me, but from mother's attitude. She insisted on *sitting* through it in a marked manner, not as though she were feeling a little faint or something, but bolt upright with firmly shut mouth, to show her disapproval. Might Heaven itself send some vague punishment? Or, still worse, would the verger speak to her?

I have wondered since those days why we all took those long walks through dull streets, and endured those long services. Not from pious or educative motives. It must have been simply for the inspiriting music that burst from that

organ and that choir. It was worth all the endurance, even of
the Litany. No footling sentimental hymns, but Te Deums,
Psalms, Creeds, Introits, and Kyries that intoxicated us.
During one boy's solo my father was so excited that his fist
came thump down on his neighbour's shoulder. We children
knew all the chants, and used often at home to converse loudly
to their tunes. We had nicknames for our favourite Creeds.
There was the 'trumpet' Creed, with six trumpet-notes on the
organ before each section. We could rely on getting this on
the great Feast days. Another was called the 'cup of tea' Creed,
because the recurring theme was just the same as that of a
comic song of the time, running:

First you take and warm your teapot, let your water boiling be,
That's a most important secret, and see you do not spare the tea.

Sermons, of course, were on the endurance side, but had
some alleviations. I had a nice long sit down, and as I was
always seated close to the pulpit I enjoyed the colours of the
marble pillars, and could weave fancies round the Punjaub,
a funny name to have on a pulpit. If the preacher grew fierce
I looked at the statue of Samveli Johnson, whom I vaguely
connected with Sam Weller, and if he were gentle I looked
at the one of Howard with his keys, a satisfying face and figure.
It is curious that during all those years I never inquired who
these people were. The sermons were seldom less than three-
quarters of an hour. To the preacher it was the chance of a
lifetime. He would never again 'address London'. We got to
be a little sorry for him as he went up the steps, conducted by
the melancholy-looking verger who certainly must have given
him a gloomy foreboding of his reception by 'London'. He
did not know how his voice would carry under the dome, and
we took joy in seeing whether he would bawl, or roar like any
sucking dove.

During the summer months we had a series of colonial
bishops, who told us all they had ever thought in their far-
flung places. The only man we ever heard more than once
was the Dean, who always preached on the great Feast days,

and let us off with half an hour. The only sermon of his that
I recall was a Christmas one, when he besought us to enjoy
ourselves, dinner and all, because that was what the Lord
would like best. 'A sprig of withered parsley' was the description of Dean Church by some wit of the day. He was a very
slight, care-worn-looking man, ending the procession into
the service, letting his board hang listlessly from his hand,
mounting into his stall with a semi-detached air, as if the whole
business was of little concern. For some reason we had bound-
less respect for him, and liked to hear him read the Gospel, in
which the only word he ever emphasized was 'and'. The effect
of this, strangely enough, was to give extraordinary dignity
to the narrative of the passion.

The sermons were usually stiff with learning and far over
our heads. After one on Solomon's vision, I asked Barnholt
on the way home whether *he* would have chosen wisdom if
he had been Solomon. 'Oh, no,' said he, 'I've got enough of
that. I should have asked for a new cricket-bat.' The rest of
the walk home was spent in enlarging on the things we might
have got from such a golden opportunity.

Dinner-time on Sunday was the occasion for us all to com-
pare notes and criticisms of the voices of canon, minor canon,
and preacher, and the shade of ritualism of the stranger.
Whether he stood at the north end of the altar, or in the middle
—it was a burning question in those days, when clergymen
were being imprisoned for Romish practices. We had no
feelings in the matter, but we loved to see some one sailing
near the wind.

The afternoons hung heavy. It seemed to be always 3 o'clock.
All amusements, as well as work, were forbidden. It was a real
privation not to be allowed to draw and paint. However, an
exception was made in favour of illuminated texts, and we
rivalled the old monks in our zeal for copying Scripture, with
the same kind of worldly decorations that they devised.

Naturally our main stand-by was reading, but here again our
field was limited by mother's notions of what was appropriate
for Sunday. *Tom Brown*, *Robinson Crusoe*, Hans Andersen's

Tales, and *Pilgrim's Progress* were permitted, but not the *Arabian Nights,* or Walter Scott, or indeed any novel. We had to fall back on bound volumes of *Good Words for the Young,* which were not so bad as the title suggests, and contained plenty of stories. Again and again I turned to something entitled *The Dark Journey,* only to find that it was an account of one's digestion. You may wonder why I did this more than once, but I always hoped that I had been mistaken, and that such a splendid title must mean a good story. No, there was still that forbidding picture of one's insides cut through the middle.

We all liked certain parts of a three-volume story called *Henry Milner,* which purported to be an account of the up-bringing of a Christian gentleman. I believe he never did anything wrong, but his school-fellows did, and all their gay activities shone like misdeeds in a pious world.

The Bible proved often more entertaining than the 'good' books. One day when Barnholt was desperate for a new story I recommended Esther as being as good as the *Arabian Nights.* He hung back, however, until I urged the point that God was not mentioned in it. 'No, really?' he cried, seized the Bible, and soon became absorbed in the plot. He and I used to gloat too over the horrors of the Revelation, more than over its brighter passages. One thing puzzled us: when the twenty-four elders had cast down their crowns, what happened next? Did they run and pick them up again to throw them down again, or were new crowns supplied to them?

Religious talk was seldom, if ever, inflicted on us. The question of conscience once arose when mother was reading *Jessica's First Prayer* aloud to Barnholt and me. 'What means by conscience?' said I. 'Surely,' mother replied in rather shocked tones, 'you have heard the voice of God speaking to you, and telling you not to do what is wrong?' Scenting danger, I hastily agreed. 'And you too, Barnholt, of course?' 'No,' said he, 'I've never heard any voice at all.' Mother pressed him, asserting that he *must* have heard it. But he stuck to his point, and how I admired him, and wished I had had the courage to say the same, because I had never heard anything either.

Sunday newspapers did exist, but were not respectable. How horrified my father was on discovering that the servants had been reading little bits to me out of *Lloyd's Weekly*! He gave me to understand that I must never read it because the small print was so bad for me. Now and again, however, I noticed on a Sunday walk that he bought a paper. For sometimes my father would cut out all church-going and announce, 'Let's go up to Hampstead Heath to see the sun shine.' We never gave him time to change his mind, or mother's conscience a chance to get to work about Sunday travelling, but were soon hustling off with him to the station. Yes, the sun was shining on the heath sure enough, and we scampered about the wild paths that stretch beneath the group of firs by the *Spaniards*. Fifty years have made little difference to that scene. I think the very bench under the trees is the same, but the country lane that led to Highgate has been civilized into villadom and a good run for cars. Down Highgate Hill we ran, always paying our respects to Dick Whittington's stone on the way, took a tram along Holloway, and reached home with the appetites of hunters.

Sometimes when the weather was particularly bad, or we had friends who jibbed at the long way to St. Paul's, we went to a church near by. Like most Londoners, we had no idea as to a parish church, but chose the one we liked best. Needless to say, this was one where the service was not intolerably dull. In fact we chose one that was considered dangerously 'high', where they 'did things'. I heard a neighbour say to mother in awful undertones (so that I should not hear), 'My dear Mrs. Thomas, they *say* he has a confessional.' Liturgical colours on the altar, Byzantine paintings on the walls, Gregorian chants, Communion more than once a month—all pointed to Rome. We children enjoyed this danger-zone and hoped that incense would be started. Charles declared he smelt it one day, but then his imagination always outran fact.

So mumbling and queer was the old vicar's delivery that he

seemed to have hot potatoes in his mouth, and none but his usual congregation could understand him. One of his sermons had a local touch and sticks in my memory. Apparently Ahab, in addition to his ordinary misdoings, had (in some obscure part of the Bible) built himself an ivory palace. This was definitely wrong, and modern men of business who were similarly extravagant would come to a similar bad end. 'You successful merchants, who build unto yourselves your ivory palaces in Highbury New Park. . . .' This puzzled me, because I knew that road from end to end, and had never noticed a house at all resembling an ivory palace. The way to escape the fate of Ahab was to place your offerings 'in the box that you will find at the door'. Charles imitated the vicar so well and so often that the joke lost its edge, but a cousin came to stay with us and supposed him to be exaggerating. When she attended the church with us, however, and the old fellow began his mouthing, she had to go hurriedly into the churchyard to let loose her laughter.

The vicar's wife paid us an occasional call, frightening me with her severity, for she wore the black cloak and hood of a nun. She said that it saved her having to think about a new dress. Mother, full of daring, attacked her one day on the sameness of her husband's sermons. She agreed that they were monotonous, and advised mother to meditate instead of listening. 'That's what I do myself,' she added. She sat in church just like other people, so I longed to ask, 'What means by meditate?', but was too overawed to ask until she had gone. The severe bearing of this man and wife hid, and had perhaps caused, a tragedy. An only child, a son, the apple of their eye, was destined for Holy Orders. But he did something disgraceful—either was seen drunk, or joined the Salvation Army, or married an impossible girl, or something. Mother's common sense might have blown away the trouble, but she had a horror of poking into other people's business unless asked. All we knew was that the boy had been forbidden to come home, and a letter to him was returned to the Post Office marked 'Not known here'. There was something dreadfully final about this, and when his poor mother told us about it she broke through her stony reserve and sobbed piteously.

There were plenty of other places of worship round the neighbourhood which the boys sampled now and then, for the sake of variety—most of them very low church, or 'crawling', as they called it. My father said he didn't care where they went as long as it wasn't a 'schism shop', by which he meant anything nonconforming. However, when Moody and Sankey were making news everywhere, mother felt a great impulse to see what it was all about. There was a meeting arranged quite near, at the Agricultural Hall I think, and off she went. Her report to the family was that everything was 'too exposed', and she had been horribly afraid that Mr. Moody would point his finger at her and ask some intimate question, or invite her to sit on the converts' bench. So she got away as soon as possible, bringing with her a fat hymn-book. Charles found this most attractive for rendering in his own fashion on the piano, and one day we found ourselves dancing a polka heartily to the tune of 'Hold the Fort'.

My father's Sunday efforts weakened towards evening, and after tea he liked to read aloud to us from books that sounded quite well, but afforded some chance of frivolity. Of course Shakespeare is Shakespeare, but we got boisterous joy out of Falstaff and his men in buckram, out of Hotspur's contempt for Glendower, and Fluellen's brush with Pistol over the leek. *Ingoldsby Legends* were always in demand, and above all the *Misadventures at Margate*, which we knew almost by heart. I took my cue from the boys and laughed whenever they did, but it was not till much later in life that I perceived the humour of what was read. Never mind, I was led to welcome a joke as though it were a jewel, and the mere habit has made life jollier. One thing over which they laughed did, however, worry me. The closing couplet of the Margate poem was so easy to understand, and so silly. How could any one be so foolish as to ring a bell, have the door answered, and then have nothing to say but that a friend of his was pretty well?

Pickwick Papers, by some blessed workings of mother's conscience, did not come under the head of novels. They were 'papers'. She herself led the laughter over the long gamekeeper and Bob Sawyer's supper-party. Not sabbatical by any means, but those readings rescued our childhood's Sundays from the grimness that might otherwise have stuck to them And often my father would read us things that he loved, without a single word of 'explanation'. Of these the *Ancient Mariner* stands out beyond the rest. O happy living things! Why do people murder them by explanations?

VIII

Callers

LONDONERS have no neighbours. During our fifteen years
in the one house we never had the slightest acquaintance
with our 'semi-detached', nor with the people round,
although we knew several by sight and gave them nicknames.
A very few became known to us through the vicar, the school-
master, and the doctor.

The doctor himself was a dear. He saw us through all our
infectious diseases and coughs, curing most of our ailments
more by jollity than physic. He was specially fond of me
because, as he frequently said, he had saved my life. I had
almost gone with measles, and when hope had practically
departed he ordered champagne. I was only six years old, but
I remember that champagne, and my father bringing it to me
in his shirt-sleeves that hot summer evening. The very word
'champagne', connected as it was with festivity, and my father's
face all smiles, put new life into me, and gave me kick enough
to pull through. But I took ages to recover, and can remember
the excitement of my first day out of bed, wrapped in a shawl
and allowed to sit in my window.

Most of our illnesses mother managed by herself. Sir William
Gull, whom she had known intimately, told her that he always
gave a patient what he asked for, even sherry in high fever if
he wanted it, because a man's stomach and appetite were the
best guides. On this simple principle we were not pressed to
swallow arrowroot and other horrors, but allowed to starve
until we called out for something.

So few were our demands on the doctor that he used to pay
mother unofficial calls, in the middle of his morning rounds.
To cheer himself up, I fancy. These visits were glory for me
because they broke into my morning's work and gave me a
chance to hear juicier bits than the ordinary visitor provided.

The mysterious undertone would excite me and impress my memory far more than a matter-of-fact style.

'You have no idea, Mrs. Thomas, how many ladies I attend whose only malady is secret bottles.'

'But how do they manage to get the stuff?'

'The grocer supplies it, and puts it down as sugar on the bills.'

'How did you find that out?'

'From a grocer patient.'

'How do you treat them?'

'Well, you see, I have my living to make, and dare not be frank with them. They would be offended and call in some one else.'

Occasionally the bits were perhaps too juicy for me to hear, however guardedly worded, and mother would tell me to run and play. Chagrined, as all children are by this speciously pleasant order, I used to carry out her instructions to the letter. My play consisted in stealing the Doctor's stethoscope from his top-hat in the hall, hiding it, and then sitting at the top of the stairs to await events. Soon would come the dramatic moment—the sound of good-byes, front door opened, seizure of gloves, and then the outcry at the missing stethoscope. 'That naughty Molly at her tricks again!' It was not until mother threatened fearful vengeance that I would run down and retrieve the poor instrument (that was glad of a change, I fancied) from behind the books or under the hearthrug. The doctor would then catch me in his arms and kiss me, thereby encouraging me to future performances. Although his beard prickled me I liked his smell, and I suppose that is why disinfectants are pleasant to me to this day.

One red-letter day he took me on his rounds. No word in the English language can express my feeling of importance. He was very solemn, and I duly lived up to it. Seated in the victoria while he was paying a visit, I was too remote, physically and mentally, to converse with the coachman, so I tried to imagine what was going on inside. When the doctor emerged from one extremely long visit I asked him what was the matter in there. Gravely he looked at me, and said, 'You must never, never, never ask a doctor what is the matter with a patient.' Silly man, he might have known that even a child can put two and two together. He should have said 'whooping-cough' and passed on. However, it was a valuable bit of professional etiquette that I thus acquired early.

As for the usual female visitors, they seemed to enjoy nothing but worries and grievances, which they poured forth on mother. Sitting in a little chair in the corner I used to amuse myself by listening to the funny sounds of the voices, high or low, now whining, now nervously giggling, but I cannot remember ever to have heard a woman visitor laugh. Sometimes I counted the number of times they said 'yes'. One visitor was grand at this, for every now and again she would let forth a chromatic scale of the word 'yes', starting on a high note and rushing down in a torrent of concession. Some visitors would make no attempt to talk at all unless mother kept hard at it. One day, in the middle of a deadly pause, I broke in brightly with,

'I know what you are thinking, mother.'

Snatching at any straw, mother was unwise enough to invite me to tell.

'You are thinking up what you can possibly say next.'

Startled, mother looked anxiously at the visitor, who fortunately was too stupid to notice anything odd in my remark.

Among the frequenters of the house was a young man named Arthur Collins. Where he came from, or by whom introduced, nobody seemed to know. He cannot have been a friend of the boys. He would look in at all hours and stay endlessly—too shy to go. He had a shock of black hair, a perpetual smile, and nothing whatever to say. Invariably during his visit he held on his knees a paper parcel, which we all knew to be a present for one of us. Never summoning up courage to give it, he would throw it on the front-door mat as he left. You may think how pleasant this must have been. But we all knew that the present would be a cardboard tidy, or bookmark, or box, ornamented with green ribbon—all his own work. The house was already littered with these gifts, so that we loathed the sight of them, and his mode of delivery involved a letter of thanks from the unlucky recipient.

He liked to join in any game that was afoot, so long as it was simple, such as dominoes or draughts, but was so good natured that he always let his opponent win. Not that he said so, but we were all aware of it, and could see him making mistakes on purpose. To poor Arthur we owed our disgust with obtrusively unselfish people, and our understanding of mother's oft-repeated maxim: 'Please yourself, your friends will like you the better.'

Dym and Barnholt had gone one day for a long tramp—train to Barnet, thence to St. Albans, and back by Potters Bar. From the outset everything went wrong. They missed the train and had a long wait to begin with. They left their parcel of sandwiches in the rack. The rain, which they laughed at when it began, increased to a steady downpour. The tea at St. Albans, on which they had counted to revive them, was only just warm and very dear. Barnholt lost his last coin, a half-crown, through a hole in his pocket, and Dym had only just enough for their fares home from Potters Bar. On the way they amused themselves with the fun they would get out of telling their misfortunes to the others, and as they neared the house they agreed that it only needed to find Arthur Collins in the study to crown the day. The servant opened the door with the words,

'Mr. Collins is in the study, sir; he has been waiting for you for some time.'

While acquaintances were few, we were richly endowed with relations, mostly aunts and cousins, whose notion of a visit involved far more than a mere hour's chat. Aunt Polly was the worst. We knew her knock, which became a signal for the boys to stampede to the study, and become deep in their work. Exceedingly fat and affectionate, she would envelop me in her embrace, and burst into fulsome flattery as to how I was 'getting on', a 'fine girl', and 'so like dear Helen' (an aunt even fatter than herself). What annoyed mother most was her habit of turning up about ten minutes before a meal, with loud declarations that she couldn't stop, had only just popped in, and must be off at once. When the meal had been delayed in accordance with this idea, she would catch a savoury smell and rearrange her mind. (As Tom used to remark, 'No *lady* smells roast chicken'.) She would think that perhaps the meal would give her a chance to see the dear boys. After that it seemed abrupt to go, and she would stay to tea, and then wait till my father came home, to see dear Tom. It often ended in his having to see her home, or, worse still, in her being put up for the night. And she revoked at whist. She used to wish that she had ten sons, 'like your wonderful and industrious boys, Mary dear'. We all heartily wished the same, for they would occupy her time completely.

Another aunt, of very different calibre, also lived within visiting range. Instead of flattering the family, she found fault. Her hobbies were correct behaviour and religion. The latter varied from the severest forms of nonconformity to extreme High Church, according to the last friend who had influenced her. The only shade of thought that never attracted her was the Broad Church, 'where, Mary dear, they do not believe in Hell'.

She lost no opportunity of improving our morals, and manners at table, feeling that poor Mary was very lax with those boys. They, needless to say, enjoyed shocking her with their adventures and stories, coloured for her benefit. During one Primitive Methodist period she markedly left behind a little magazine, containing a list of 'persons for whom our prayers are requested'. Charles, always on the scent for the ridiculous, seized the list hopefully, and hooted with delight when he found: 'For a family of four boys and one girl. That they may be led to give up their frivolous mode of life.'

'That's us,' he shouted, and we all crowded round to see ourselves in print, but not in the spirit that Aunt Lizzie had intended.

Among several of her gifts to me was a little book of devotion, called *The Narrow Way*. I tried hard to cope with its suggestions, but it had no pictures, and endless prayers for every occasion. Let alone grace at meals, you were to say a prayer on hearing a clock strike, on waking up in the night, on receiving bad news, and even on taking medicine. Now medicine was bad enough in itself, and I concluded that no one could really be as good as this book wanted and that it was a fearful waste of time.

On one of my bad days I refused to finish up my rice pudding, was sent from the room, and fled in angry tears to my bedroom. Soon Aunt Lizzie came up to me with the information that 'it says in the Bible that the disobedient are to burn for ever in the Lake of Fire, with idolaters and murderers and liars'. This sounded all too likely, and without questioning the accuracy of her quotation I went back and choked down that rice pudding.

Another distasteful point about this aunt was her regular visit once a week to give Charles and me our music lessons. No child of to-day would believe the long hours we spent practising. I had to hold my hand so flat that a penny would not fall off, and then hammer down finger after finger on the piano. What misery the third finger gave me! Then followed scales and more exercises, and last of all a little 'piece' which I loathed most of all. The only thing I really enjoyed was the chromatic scale, walking down the piano and playing every note, as fast as I could.

In spite of the fun that we made of Aunt Lizzie we were really fond of her, because she never gushed and would do anything for us. And we all knew her tragedy. She had run away to be married, and her husband had turned out a drunken brute with no redeeming attraction. He tortured her to such an extent that she was obliged to flee from lodging to lodging to avoid him, and to make a living for herself by giving music lessons. It is no wonder that she took gloomy views of life, and had such vivid ideas of Hell. Victorian times are supposed to have been so settled and happy and care-free, but my recollections hardly tally with this rosy picture. Surely to-day no woman would endure such humiliations year after year.

But then, of course, Lizzie's extreme piety may have driven her husband to drink and extreme measures.

The unrelieved melancholy of a third aunt must have arisen from a lifelong boredom. Unlike Polly who was an old maid, and Lizzie who was unhappily married and childless, Bessie had a kind husband and three children. But never did she rejoice. A watery smile of politeness was her utmost effort. A tear seemed always about to fall, more depressing than a burst of crying. When the boys had decamped as usual to the study, 'Oh, Mary,' she would say, fixing mother with one eye at a time, and in an undertone as though disclosing a state secret, 'how I wish that I had never married.' Of course I hoped for the worst, and each time imagined that some dark story must lie behind so much misery. But no, mother used to assure me afterwards that there was nothing wrong with her beyond self-pity. It's true that her husband was called Bertie, and my father said he was an awful fool, but beyond these drawbacks there was nothing amiss.

The cousins that came every now and again belonged to that vague area of distant relationship included by the Cornish under the word 'cousin'. They were of all ages, and the more elderly ones had to be addressed as 'Cousin Jane', 'Cousin Henry', and so on. One large family of parents and grown-up offspring used to come to see us in small groups. We had some trouble in keeping their names and peculiarities clear. They never came without the tidings that one of them had passed away, and we were naturally anxious not to ask after his health at their next visit. At last Charles discovered that whereas they always put 'dear' in front of every name, they gave any one who had passed away the extra title of 'poor dear'.

Amid all these lugubrious kinsfolk and acquaintance, mother found her social duties tiresome enough, and liked to have me in the room in order that she might give vent to her feelings afterwards. 'Molly dear,' she would exclaim, 'I must say what I think about Aunt Lizzie, or I shall burst.' Charles enabled us to bear a lot by means of his deadly imitations of every one. But mother, the gayest of mortals, had to rack her brains to get the conversation away from grievances. She even asked a visitor one day how she managed to have such an effective bustle. The astounding answer was '*The Times*. I find its paper so good, far more satisfactory than the *Daily News*', and putting her hand under her skirt she tore off a piece to show us.

One last acquaintance I must mention—an old lady who was too great an invalid to go out. Mother used to take me now and again to see her. Her name was Mrs. Ayres. She wore a larger cap than the usual kind that middle-aged ladies used to put on when they took their hats off. 'Where is Mr. Ayres?' I asked mother one day, when we got outside. 'There isn't any Mr. Ayres,' she replied, 'and there never was any Mr. Ayres.' After a mysterious pause she added, 'They call her Mrs. Ayres from courtesy, because she is so old.'

Who were 'they'? I pictured people gathering together round a green table and deciding, 'Let's call Miss Ayres Mrs. Ayres.' But to this day I have wondered at what particular moment this decision was made.

IX

A Long Railway Journey

OUR lack of interest in kinsfolk and acquaintance in London was more than balanced by our enthusiasm for our relations in Cornwall.

Mother's family was not only numerous and well-to-do, but intelligent and jolly. Hardly a year passed but some of us paid them a visit, and occasionally it was all of us. Among, then, the bits of luck in my childhood must be included this plunge from London to the depth of the country.

To us children an important element in this piece of luck was the journey of three hundred miles that it involved. Our parents must have thought otherwise. Had they not been peculiarly care-free by disposition they would never have embarked on the adventure of taking five children all that way in a train of the 'seventies. Coaching days were doubtless bad, but there were inns on the way.

We used to go to bed earlier the day before, not so much to please mother as to bring to-morrow a bit sooner. We got up long before it was necessary, impeding all the sandwich-making and hard-boiling of eggs that was going on. But eat a good breakfast we could not, being 'journey-proud', as our old cook used to express our excited state. Meanwhile the luggage was being assembled in the hall, having its last touches of cording and labels. For weeks I had been packing in my bedroom, and once I presented five large cardboard boxes, wobbly with various belongings. My father ran upstairs to inspect them, and solemnly looking at them said, 'Now, Molly, which of these is really the most important?' Charmed by his business-like manner and by the word 'important', I gladly pointed to one, and consented to leave the others behind.

The next crisis was the fetching of a cab. At 7 o'clock in the morning there was no certainty of getting one quickly, and we kept rushing to the window until some one shouted, 'Here it comes.' If you saw that cab to-day your anxiety would be as to whether it could possibly stay the course to Paddington. The few 'growlers' still to be seen in the London streets are royal coaches compared with those of the 'seventies. They were like the omnibuses, with the same dingy blue velvet, only much dirtier, and as they were used for taking people to hospitals my father used to call them 'damned fever-boxes'. To us children, no Cinderella's fairy-carriage could have been handsomer than the cab actually at the door. If we were all going my father and the elder boys had to follow in a second cab. Luggage was piled on the top, and we were packed in among rugs, umbrellas, and hand-bags. At last the cabby climbed up to his seat and whipped up the horse. It took an hour or more to jog along from Canonbury to Paddington, but we did reach the enchanted spot at last.

The train was scheduled to start at 9 a.m. and to arrive at Camborne at 9 p.m. This was before the days of the Flying Dutchman, not to mention the Cornishman and the Riviera Express. Even when the Flying Dutchman was begun it had no third class, and was too expensive for the whole family. Luncheon-baskets had not been invented, neither was it possible to reserve seats. In order, therefore, to travel all together in one compartment we had to arrive more than half an hour before the train was to start. There was then the suspense of waiting for it to come in, and my fear that we might not be on the right platform or that the Great Western had forgotten all about it. My father meanwhile was taking the tickets and having the luggage labelled. Never did he hasten his steps or hurry, no matter what the emergency, so that there was the additional fear that he would miss the train. When at last we were all safely in a carriage, he would saunter off to buy a paper, and other people were coming in.

In time everything was settled and we were gliding out, 'with our faces towards Cornwall', as mother used to say. Very little of the view from the windows escaped us, and I was privileged to 'kneel up' and report the latest news to the company. No sooner had we fairly left London behind, were gathering speed, and had sated ourselves with fields and hedges for a while, than we began to survey our fellow passengers and make friends with them. In the old broad-gauge carriages there were usually six a side, and much courtesy was needed for a long run when there was no escape from one another. Our parents took care to found a family tradition of being good travellers, which was understood to mean that we must not be a nuisance to other people, by crowding the window, talking loudly, moving about, eating before the appointed time (and perhaps being ill) . . . and the evil-doings of children who began to eat sweets before Reading were pointed out.

Where we came out strong in the carriage company at large was in our superior familiarity with the route. We knew all the points of interest to be looked out for. 'We are going to Cornwall.' 'We always go there,' 'We'll show you when it comes.' By such delicate expressions of superiority we managed to conceal our contempt for the poor creatures who 'were only going to Bristol', or some degraded person who had to 'change at Didcot'. What we most liked was a grown-up, preferably a man, who was a complete stranger to the line. A kindly clergyman would listen with apparent fervour to our informative talk about Brunel and the viaducts, or be shown the 'very place that Turner took for his "Rain, Steam and Speed"'. We knew the exact point to get a view of Windsor Castle, and showed it as if it were our own.

Reading, the first stop, was great fun for those on the near side. What more cheering than to see distracted people looking for seats when we were definitely full up? If we had a vacant seat at any stop Charles would suggest that I should be pushed forward, for any one on seeing me, he maintained, would try farther on. Or he would ejaculate, as any one was about to come in, 'No one would think that Barnholt was recovering from measles!' We talk of the confusion of a modern station, but it is orderly peace compared to the rushing about and shouting of those days. The wonder is that we ever moved on again. And yet we didn't dare to leave the carriage, because at any moment the guard might decide that he had had enough.

Didcot had one definite pleasure. We knew that little boys would be going up and down the platform singing out, 'Banbury cakes! Banbury cakes!' And mother would crane out and buy some, just to encourage the crew.

Next came Swindon—name of sweet assurance. How often mother used to say, 'They *can't* leave Swindon under ten minutes, no matter how late we are.' Considering our early breakfast, or lack of it, the refreshment-room at Swindon was a land of Canaan, and the hot soup all round is still a joyful memory. So hot it was that Dym launched a theory that it was hoped some would be left to serve up for the next train. Those ever-memorable ten minutes were no doubt entirely for the gain of the restaurant and entirely to the detriment of the Great Western, but they were sheer life-savers to long-distance travellers. In later years the railway had to compensate the restaurant for doing away with those ten minutes, to the tune of £50,000. Perhaps a little remorseful, the restaurant proprietors presented a silver model engine to Swindon, to commemorate the transaction, and the little model is known to the railwaymen as 'the £50,000 engine'.

Thus refreshed we were all agog for our next excitement— the Box Tunnel. The railway cuttings grew higher and higher, and at last we rushed with a piercing whistle into the total darkness of 'the longest tunnel in the world'. The oil lamps, and later the gas lamps, were let down from above with much labour only at dusk. There was no thought of lighting up for a tunnel. Old ladies may have been afraid of robbery and murder, but it was a great feature of the day's entertainment to us. By a pre-arranged plan the boys and I rose stealthily and felt our way into one another's places. When the train emerged into the light the elders sustained a turn, or handsomely pretended that they did.

The charm of Bristol was its appearance of being a half-way house. Not that it was so by any means, but it was the elbow-joint in the journey. The muddle and rush were greater even than at Reading, and we were often kept there for some twenty minutes. Yet we dared not leave the carriage for more than a mere leg-stretch just outside the door. I sucked much pleasure from hanging out at the off-side window, to watch the man tapping the wheels and applying the yellow stuff from his box. Thus I understood what my father meant by calling London butter 'train-oil'.

Some of our company usually left the train at Bristol, so that we had the carriage more or less to ourselves, and could move about more freely. This was specially desirable because there was soon to come a magic moment when a glimpse of the sea was possible, just for the short time when Bridgwater Bay was visible on our right. Then we bowled along the warm sleepy country-side of Somerset, with no excitements beyond fields and cows and tiny villages, mile after mile. This was the strategic point that mother chose for unveiling dinner. A bulging basket had long been eyed as it sat in the rack. Restaurant cars are boons, and luncheon-baskets have their merry surprises, but for food as a species of rapture nothing compares with sandwiches, eggs, pasties, and turnovers, doled out one by one from napkins, when the supply is severely limited. Oranges in summer were unknown then, as well as all the foreign apples and other fruit to be had in London to-day. We had to slake our thirst with acid-drops and a tiny ration of lemonade. If by any chance a fellow passenger remained we always managed to do some little barter of biscuits or sweets, because strange food is even more pleasant than one's own.

We used to hail Exeter as being 'almost there', for it was in Devon, actually the next county to Cornwall, and definitely 'west'. A quiet dignity pervaded its saintly stations, but we could never stay long because of course we were late. A train in those days was never 'on time'. After Exeter we were all keyed up for the greatest treat of the journey. I have travelled in many show places of Europe and America, but have never been along a piece of line to equal the run from Exeter to Teignmouth. We children were not stirred as mother was by the beauties of the estuary and the opposite shore. What we looked out for were the waders carrying on some mysterious hunt in the water, and two pleasure-boats, shaped like some kind of water-fowl, and called the *Swan* and *Cygnet*. I never dreamt but what they were real birds.

Then, with a magnificent gesture, the Great Western swept us to the sea-side, indeed almost into the sea. Mother remembered a day when the waves had washed into the carriage. The bare possibility of such a thing made this part of the run something of an adventure, and we almost hoped it would happen again.

The sun was always shining at Dawlish, and there was the sea all spread out in dazzling blue. And as if the train knew how to enhance the effect, it would roll in and out of short tunnels in the 'rouge', or red sandstone of Devon. Each time it emerged the sea looked bluer and the rocks more fantastic in shape. However beautiful the inland scenery might be, it seemed dull after this, and after Teignmouth we usually fell asleep. I remember being laid out at length with my head on mother's lap, and the rest being a blank till the glad sound of 'Here's Plymouth' woke me.

By now it was late afternoon, and you would suppose that here at last would be some chance of tea and a wash in comfort. Ah no! The London train didn't care about Cornwall, there were no through carriages arranged for long-distance people, and we had to change into a local affair, with hard wooden seats, and patronized by a succession of market people with large bundles. By the time we had found this train, seen the luggage shifted, carried along our small parcels, and settled into our seats, there was no time to do more than buy a bag of buns. They had not thought then of allowing people to carry cups of tea into the carriage with them.

In all this confusion I had time to notice that we were coming out of Millbay the same way that we had gone in. It was a sort of terminus, apparently, and very mysterious, because I was assured that we were not going back to London. I asked my father what became of the engine that had brought us from London. How did it get out so as to pull the train away again? He explained very carefully how it was lowered into an underground passage, run along under the train, and then hauled up again at the other end. This seemed to me no more peculiar than most things.

Shipping on the Hamoaze amused us mightily enough until we reached the climax of our journey—the Albert Bridge. We were leaving 'England' behind and were in the enchanted land of Cornwall at last. We greeted the tiny whitewashed cottages of the 'natives' with far greater fervour than we had shown over Windsor Castle. We vied with one another in trying to remember the order in which the stations came. We stopped at all of them. And when I say stopped I mean stopped. There was none of the hurry of Reading or Bristol. We leant out to catch the accents of the porter, proclaiming his piece in the soft west-country drawl. We watched all the greetings and partings and waving of hands of the travellers. . . . Then would descend that peculiar silence of a country station that signifies that every one is settled, and the guard feels that it is safe to let the train start again.

If a sun-bonneted market woman got in with us mother could never resist talking to her, and answering the invariable Cornish question 'Wheer be 'ee goin'?' Then would follow the astonished 'From Lunnon, are 'ce? Aw, my deer!'

And now it was growing dusk, and the familiar tin-mine buildings were silhouetted against the sky, and generally darkness had descended before we ran into Camborne more than an hour late. We had become indescribably dirty and tired and hungry. But our reception atoned for all. Countless uncles and aunts and cousins were crowding the platform, and as we got out every one was exclaiming 'Here they are!' We children were the heroes and the spoilt darlings of the hour. We were bundled into waiting carriages and driven to a royal spread. On one such occasion I remember my cousin Edgar running all the mile and a half by the side of the carriage in the dark, giving us a whoop of joy when a gate into a lane had to be opened for us to pass.

X

Reskadinnick

SUCH was the name of the homestead that was our journey's
end. To any but a Cornishman the word sounds strange.
London tradespeople made curious play with it, and Peter
Robinson once sent a parcel to my aunt addressed: 'Miss
Vivian, c/o Rev. Kadinnick.' To us children the name was
synonymous with Paradise.

I call it a homestead because it was much more than a mere
home or house or farm. When the town was left behind you
entered a lane through a gate. This had the alluring name of
Blackberry Lane, and meandered between mossy hedges thick
with wild flowers until a large white gate barred the way.
Beyond this was a quarter of a mile of sweeping drive, bordered
by neatly cut grass and tall trees of great variety with more
woodland behind them. Here and there was a bright flowering
shrub, and in one recessed spot was a deep pond among the
trees. A beautiful cool walk on a summer's day, but terrifying
at night when one had to come home alone in the dark.

With the last curve of the drive the house came in sight,
facing a large lawn, bordered by wooded banks and dotted
with huge elms. While the carriage-drive led away through
another wood to a lane beyond, a flower-garden lay on the
other side of the house. Over a little brook and up a sunny
bank there stretched a kitchen garden with fruit-trees in-
numerable, and in another part was a special orchard.

My grandfather had planned the whole place and planted
all the trees except two Scotch firs in the drive, of unknown
antiquity. The house too was of his own building, arranged
for his bride in the reign of George III.

He had started with a farm and its dwelling-house, with
huge old outside chimneys, gables, rafters, and stone floors.
The walls were made of anything to be had some two or three

centuries ago—mostly mud and timber. In some alterations made during my time a large trunk of a tree was found embedded in one wall. In some places these walls were two yards thick, and it had been customary to gouge a bit out when a cupboard was wanted.

At the end of this old part he had built a new Georgian house, with pillared front and a brick arch at each side, concealing the back regions. These arches became mellowed in colour and creeper-clad, and gave a pleasant surprise to any one approaching and passing through to the beautiful older buildings beyond.

The connexion of the new house with the old had necessitated some strange staircases and dark corners, and every room seemed to lead into some other room. And it was easy to get on the roof, or jump from a window at almost any point. The delightfully rambling *ensemble* seemed to have been designed by some celestial architect for the sole purpose of playing hide-and-seek. My grandfather had ten children, and no doubt they took as much advantage of this as we grandchildren did.

The out-buildings were even more rambling and mysterious than the interior. Beyond the great dairy there was the hen-yard, surrounded by coops inhabited by hens in every stage of their duty. From this you went into the big yard, with its long row of stables and a granary over them. Beyond this again was the lower yard, where the cows were housed and milked in sheds all round, and where the pigs wallowed about in the middle. By the side of this was the big barn, and beyond that the 'mowey', another yard where the ricks were built up on stone supports to keep the rats away. The little lane led in one direction to the smithy, the horse-pond, and a few scattered cottages, and in the other direction to the water-mill. All round were the various fields belonging to the farm, some with cows, some with sheep, but most of them with corn.

The difficulty on arriving from London was to know where to begin enjoying oneself. I well remember one such evening, being far too excited to sleep, I kept leaping from my bed to the

window-seat, from sheer exuberance. At last I burst one of
the panes in pieces. My golden aunt thought this quite a
natural thing to do, and 'it saved having to open the window'.

As a regular thing so far as I was concerned the first charge
on the estate was a personal visit to every animal. Cats first.
These were divided into four distinct classes, and the cats
seemed to be as snobbish as humans. The parlour cats were
Persians, sat on laps and best chairs, and would never recline
in the kitchen, although they would stroll casually about when
a savoury smell was prevailing. The kitchen cats seemed to
be always having kittens in the fathomless linen-cupboard at
the top of the stairs. If they ventured into the dining-room
it was to hide under the table in the hope of gain. Orchard
cats prowled round the yards and stables, quite self-supporting,
never venturing indoors unless under stress of hunger. One
of these, a tom called Sarah, was so fierce that I was afraid to
stroke him, and threw scraps to him at a distance. Then there
were the office cats. The 'office' was a side wing of the old
house, where accounts were kept and where the farm-men used
to be paid on a Saturday. Behind it was a place called the
'slaughter-house', which I never had the courage to explore;
the name put me off. A few cats, lean and humble-minded,
managed to exist in this borderland, despised by both parlour
and kitchen cats.

The only creature that really frightened me was the turkey-
cock. Nothing in my life has ever made me so weak with
terror as that horrible gobbling bird. Tired of parading with
his harem in the orchard, he would now and again strut in
the hen-yard or mowey. He would definitely forbid me to
cross a yard if he was in it. If I made a dash to cross it, so
would he. . . .

There was never any alarm to me about a horse, and the
very smell of the stables was intoxicating. Beautiful, glossy-
coated carriage-horses, a pony for us to ride, and numberless
farm-horses—all were beloved. One of these last was called
Taffy, an enormous fellow, noted for his ferocity. At dinner
one day I was missing, and as children never fail to turn up

at meal-time unless something has gone wrong, a search was ordered. I could be found in none of the usual haunts, and as I was only five years old, anxiety began. At last I was discovered seated cross-legged, with complete unconcern, under Taffy, who was munching from his manger. The stable-boy who accidentally found me had to entice me away, for he was afraid to go near Taffy himself.

Only one dog do I remember. I think he was so dear to every one that when he died the family could never bear to have another. Theo was a great shaggy Newfoundland, who joined in all our childish games as well as ever he could, being treated as a member of the family. The old cook was heard to say one day, as she stooped to pick up his dish, 'Have you finished, please, Master Theo?' Barnholt once offered him a bite of his bun, but Theo did not quite understand the limits implied in the word 'bite', and the whole bun disappeared.

With such profusion of cows, sheep, pigs, poultry, and vegetation of all kinds, Reskadinnick was practically self-supporting, and my grandfather was able to boast frequently that there was nothing on the dinner-table but what he had produced on the farm. Fish was a rare treat, and a gift of trout or salmon was prepared and served with a ritual almost religious. Now and again there would resound from the lane a penetrating cry of 'Pilchards! Pilchards!' There had been a big haul, and a pony-cart was going round the country-side to sell them. All other food-preparations were then set aside for a pilchard orgy. The staple food was 'pig-meat' in its endless variety, and poultry. We had an old cookery-book containing this, to a London mind, extraordinary hint: 'If you have nothing in the house, and company should come, take a cold turkey, &c.' To suggest the killing and cooking of a live turkey is reasonable enough, but to select a cold one from one's 'empty' larder!

Bread was made every day, in batches of a dozen manchet loaves. A 'manchet' was a loaf moulded by hand, and not put in a tin. It was against ancient ritual for a loaf that had been cut to be placed on the table. My aunt was so angry one day when this occurred that I began to wonder what became of all the bread that was left. However, the mystery was solved when I saw her preparing a mash for the turkeys. In my day German yeast was used, but mother told me that when she was little they had no yeast, but used a bit of the dough of the previous batch to raise the new batch. What puzzled her so much was how they ever *began* it. Probably she asked and no one knew, for like so many Cornish customs it may have been centuries old, and I picture the Phoenicians bringing a piece of dough as a capital invention of the East. They used to bake the loaves, mother told me, by placing them in the wood-ash on the great stone slab in the kitchen. The stone slab is still there, and I have often stood on it and looked up the great chimney to the open sky. How jolly, I thought, those old wood fires must have been, with their spits and their cauldrons, so much more fun than the iron range, which in its turn seems fun compared to my modern efficient gas-stove.

The centre of excitement in the food scheme was the dairy. Its stone floor and slate shelves made it cool on the hottest day. On the shelves were ranged vast pans of milk, in various stages from cow to consumer. Foaming in from the milking-sheds, standing for the cream to rise before being scalded, scalded and thick with the deep cream waiting to be skimmed (the most attractive form), scalded and allowed to be drunk *ad lib.*, sold to children at the door for a halfpenny a quart, or more often given to them for nothing. Now I had a special and private permit from my aunt to go into the sacred dairy and help myself to the clotted cream whenever I liked.

The bulk of the cream was, of course, turned into butter. Turned, not churned. A churn was never seen at Reskadinnick. It had been heard of, and actually used by my aunt who lived up in the town, but Tony, my golden aunt of Reskadinnick, tossed her head at the idea. She had her own ritual of butter-making, and many a time I used to curl up in the corner of the kitchen window-seat to watch it. Her hands had to be elaborately washed first, and dipped in cold water to be cool. The wooden tub with the cream in it had to be held at a special angle on her lap. With fixed eye and stern mouth she then began to swirl the cream round, and you mustn't speak to her till the butter 'came'. One day I was allowed as a great treat to make a little butter all by myself, with no one even watching. When it 'came', behold, it was very good, and the joy of creation was mine.

Disapproval, of course, among the severer grown-ups. It was mad to let the child try such things. She might have wasted it all. But Tony was all for letting the children do and see and try things. I was wakened one night by a figure standing over me with a candle. It was Tony. 'Come along,' said she, picking me up and carrying me out pick-a-back, 'we are going to see the glow-worms.' And sure enough she carried me along the drive in my nightdress, to a spot where the worms were shining, and the elders gathered round admiring them. The child didn't catch her death, as was gloomily hoped by the disapproving, but lived to be always grateful for that only chance that has ever come her way of seeing a glow-worm.

Sanitation was not known at Reskadinnick, neither earth nor water nor any such thing. A huge tub collected the rain-water, of which there was never any shortage, and in this we washed. I had never seen a bathroom, even in London, let alone in Cornwall. A tin bath was kept in each bedroom. In the rain-water was a good deal of live stock wriggling about, but we got used to this. Our drinking-water was grand, coming from a spring in the lane.

Windows were made to open more or less, but they didn't matter much, because all through the day everybody was in and out at the ever-open doors, and in the evening when the family settled down 'to unbend over a book' every opening was shut tight. 'Night air' and 'such a draught' were considered 'enough to breed the cholera'. Our light was from candles and paraffin-lamps. Mother told me how magical it seemed to her when she first came to London to see some one turn a tap and produce a light at once from gas. She had heard how the 'best' people in London stood out against gas as being vulgar, and that Grosvenor Square was the last place to adopt it.

In spite of primitive conditions and stuffy nights, no one ever seemed to be ill. I never saw a doctor there, or heard the name of one, or heard mother speak of one in earlier days. The older people all lived to great ages, and Uncle Bill reached a hundred. Up to his last few days he could swing along without a stick. He had travelled extensively, even to Greenland, but was born and died at Reskadinnick.

All this travelling of Uncle Bill and my grandfather was for mine-prospecting. Farming was not their main interest. Tin was everything, and it was as tin-mine managers and large shareholders that they made their wealth; and the management of the farm fell to a younger son, Joe.

The chief person round whom the whole establishment revolved was my aunt, always called Tony. Ever since her mother's death she had been mistress of the house. Not only did she manage every detail of the dairy, the poultry, and the work of the servants, but she was also widely read, an accomplished musician, a witty letter-writer, and above all an entrancing teller of stories. Her peculiar charm consisted in her greater delight in the doings of others than in her own. We children loved her, I think, better than our own mother.

It was from mother that I learnt her story. Among my grandfather's travels was a visit to Norway, in connexion with a purchase of timber for the mines. He took with him, just for the fun of it, his two eldest girls, my mother and Tony. The port for Norway had to be reached by coach, and this, with the putting up at inns and the voyage in a sailing-vessel, provided plenty of adventure. Their host was a Norwegian named Barnholt, a timber-merchant on a large scale, with one son, named Otto. The visit was made the occasion for excursions up country, mountaineering, driving, riding, and sailing on the fjords. When the time came for the return to Cornwall Otto had lost his heart to Tony.

Not long afterwards Otto's father died, leaving him to carry on the business of trading with England in timber. Nothing ever went wrong with his vessel, and in his anxiety to be a little richer before his marriage he stopped paying the insurance. On the very next voyage she was lost. Utterly broken in spirit Otto died soon afterwards, and Tony never got over her grief. She had plenty of admirers and appeared to enjoy life to the full, but froze up if any one approached the idea of marriage. All her wealth of affection was poured out on us children, and more especially on Barnholt, who was Otto's godson. She was the familiar friend, too, of all the cottage children for miles around, who would do anything for 'Miss Tony'. She had learnt to speak Norsk, and taught me to repeat little verses in it. It was one of my greatest treats to come into her bedroom and be shown some of the endless treasures she had collected. Among these was a baby shoe of Barnholt's with a hole worn in its sole.

I may add here that she lived to old age, full of humour and gaiety to the last. But shortly before her death she mentioned casually in a letter to me that the one thing she could never thank God for was her creation. I understood then how much a woman can hide.

Some years before my memory runs, Uncle Bill had brought his wife and three children back to Reskadinnick to stay, and there they remained permanently. So there was no lack of inmates. My special chum was Wilhelmina, or Mina, a girl of my own age. Mina's mother was an aunt of the severe type, in whose presence we were reticent about our escapades. Aunt Knight feared accidents, feared improprieties, feared (of all the absurdities) ill effects from non-stop apple-eating. One thing I shall never forgive her to my dying day: she got wind that Mina and I were riding home from a field on the top of the hay-wagons, and forbade it with such gestures of horror that we were actually alarmed into obedience. For us the wine of life was spilt for the whole hay season. However, she could be kindness itself when things went really wrong. When some little accident did occur, it was just as she had predicted, and one of her rare smiles appeared as she brought forth bandages and things. One day my pony, empty-saddled, came galloping home along the drive. A stirrup had broken and I had been thrown. Aunt Knight looking out of the window straightway swooned, and had to be given restoratives in early Victorian style. Her handwriting was exactly like Queen Victoria's, and she always crossed her letters. She swept about in black silk, had texts hung up in her bedroom, and shook her head with disapproval at any gaiety. I made Tony laugh by telling her that Aunt Knight was like Dogberry: 'If a merry meeting may be wished, God prohibit it.' As for a funeral anywhere about, it was nuts and figs, she was sure to have heard a dog howl, an owl hoot, or a bird flutter in the chimney, and consequently knew that something would happen. If Sirius were shining brightly it meant that Hell was very full.

Christianity did not seem to have penetrated Cornwall much. The Wesleyans were full of salvation and blood, but respectable Church people upheld Old Testament morality, with only lip-service to the New. Tony told me one day that she thought the New Testament was very dull compared to the Old. One Victorian custom which my father (God bless him!) had never even contemplated, was always observed at Reskadinnick. Family prayers, which my dear old grandfather had treated sketchily, were carried out by Uncle Bill with relentless thoroughness. Instead of mumbling a few simple requests to the Almighty, as grandpapa did, he acquired a book which covered the whole nation in its petitions, and even, on Fridays, went the length of praying for foreigners. All the servants were assembled, and it was morning *and* evening. As Lord Melbourne remarked, religion was threatening to invade the sanctity of private life. Perhaps he referred to Wesleyanism, for I must say that we had no more thrust upon us, except going to church on Sunday. In spite of Uncle Bill's long prayers, I heard him say one day that he thought it *wrong* to pray for anything except courage to meet whatever came.

Our parish church was at Penponds, a village some two miles away. The dear old parson was a survival of the eighteenth-century type, who took his duties lightly. His sermons were so few that Tony said she knew them all by heart and needn't attend to them. This was as well, for her energy was completely absorbed in keeping the school children decently behaved. To us London children the whole service seemed light comic opera after the austerities of St. Paul's. Of course we never had the Litany, and the old chap would gabble through the alternate verses of the Psalms as fast as he could, followed by the hurried mumblings of the little congregation. All was simple and quickly over. On Communion Sunday (a very rare affair) matters were equally simple. Tom once 'stayed', and heard the pop of the cork as the parson opened the bottle of wine just before it was wanted.

Sundays on the whole were very jolly in Cornwall, if it hadn't been for the best clothes and the wearing of gloves. On account of these we couldn't pursue the usual plan of walking along the tops of the hedges. To those who don't know Cornwall I must explain that the hedges there are made of stones and earth, are thick with wild flowers, ivy, and ferns, and are just wide enough on the top to allow any one to walk unsteadily. Mina and I used to take one each side of a lane, and race each other along. Naturally this involved several falls and scrambling up again—not the best thing for Sunday clothes.

In the afternoons we unbelted and lay under the trees with any books we could find. My eldest cousin Beatrice was serious-minded like her mother, and attempted now and again to hold a Sunday School, and teach Mina and me something out of the Bible. But out of doors, as of course we were, the Bible somehow seemed funny, and the idea petered out.

In addition to the uncles, aunts, and cousins already mentioned there was another large family in the town about two miles away, and the coming and going was so unremitting that one hardly knew who belonged where. Sometimes even before breakfast a detachment of Uncle Joe's children would be seen coming round the last bend of the drive, full of expectancy that there would be something up.

And there always was.

XI

Outdoor Doings

'D'ESS me! D'ess me now! D'ess me *deckly* now!' According to tradition these were my words, accompanied by a stamp of my foot, as I stood at the top of the stairs one morning in my nightdress. I had overslept for once, and was frantic at having missed an hour of life. Not a moment's boredom did any of us know, but our programme depended a lot on the weather. Uncle Bill had a trying habit of tapping a kind of clock in the hall and telling us that it was going down. It surely must have gone up sometimes, in order to go down so persistently, but he never reported it. Then some wise grown-up would openly rejoice: rain was good for the garden or the tin-streams or something. However, by and by would come Uncle Joe on his horse, with a broad smile and distinct observations of blue sky in the right quarter.

Enough for us, and the glad cry of 'cliffs' would go round. Within an hour of the children's fiat Tony had packed our baskets, having duly looked round to see how many heads to count. Pretty heavy those baskets were, for in addition to the dinner they contained sketching-materials, bathing-gowns and towels, and often a book or two. However, the boys took it in turn to carry them, and the girls took sticks, spratting-hooks, and cans for possible treasures.

In twos and threes we straggled along our two-mile walk to the cliffs, a gradual rise all the way, chiefly across fields. We had no glimpse of the sea at any time until we were right at the top of the cliffs. We generally ran the last hundred yards or so, impatient for the glory that we knew to be there for us. That last lap was along a grassy path running through a stretch of purple heather. Then we saw the sea. Not the tame affair that you get at the 'sea-side', but a vast expanse of ultramarine and emerald, and far, far below, the roar of the breakers booming in and dashing their foam against the dark rocks, and the white flashing of the sea-gulls screaming to welcome us.

However, we were not there to admire—we were for the sea itself. And how to get down there? Had we been strangers we should have been afraid to attempt such a precipitous descent, but none of us could remember a time when it was not as familiar and friendly as the drive. We all plunged at once down a narrow path, a mere sheep-track, among the rocks and heather, scrambling and slithering and sliding, clutching at bushes or digging our spratting-hooks into the earth, till we reached at last a big platform of rock, from which we made a triumphal leap into the deep, soft sand.

Fortunately grown-ups never came with us, or they would have had heart-attacks, or, worse still, would have kept warning us not to slip. Our fearlessness was our safety. Once within a few yards of the sea, our things were off in a twinkling, and into the great pools we splashed. No one dreamt of venturing into that boiling, thundering, open sea, for its perils were too obvious. After about an hour of playing games in the pools, jumping from rock to rock, collecting anemones, shells, and seaweed for our cans, we clothed ourselves again, all except our feet which were bare till the final climb, and flocked round my eldest cousin, Beatrice, who dispensed the dinner. Our first course was always a pasty. I wonder who invented that perfectly complete and portable meal: a round of pastry doubled over contained fresh rump steak, and slices of potato well seasoned, and when baked became a juicy blend, but not too juicy to be grasped in the hand and nibbled away bit by bit, requiring neither knife nor fork. Then we all chased away to find a jolly place to sit, or to go on pursuing our private ends. Thirst soon brought us to Beatrice again, who doled out lemonade or cider. Then there was seed-cake for the still hungry, and plenty of apples.

After this we usually paddled and scrambled our way among the boulders to the next place along the shore that gave a possibility of climbing up again. About half-way up we would rest on some grassy shelf of the cliffs and follow our particular bent. Charles and Beatrice and I did some painting, others would merely watch the sea for distant steamers. No boats of any kind could come near that coast. My cousin Lucy had a passion for the sea, and never forgave Providence for not making her a boy. She had several blue-jackets to whom she wrote every month in connexion with Miss Weston's Mission, and from their replies she would spin us yarns, or tell us bits out of *Tom Cringle's Log*, and incidentally teach us nautical phrases and how to tie knots.

After the last lap of our long climb to the top we used to enjoy walking along the grassy path among the heather that skirted the edge of the cliff, every now and again dangerously near. At one point this led to 'Hell's Mouth', quite the most attractive spot in the world. It was a deep cove that could not be approached from the shore, and into which no boat could enter without being dashed to pieces. We used to crawl up to the overhanging edge on all fours, lie full length, and gloat with fearful pleasure at the scene below, where the great waves would swirl in on their ugly business, and presently dash out with triumphant roar and splash of spray. Lucy had blood-curdling tales of human bones down there, of people who had fallen down, or, more darkly, been pushed. I have had to come away hurriedly, understanding Horatio's words:

> *The very place puts toys of desperation*
> *Without more motive into every brain*
> *That looks so many fathoms to the sea*
> *And hears it roar beneath.*

On the way home we wandered about the fields, gathering any spoil we could find to take home to Tony—blackberries, mushrooms, wild flowers. She welcomed everything, but her first demand was always, 'Show me your sketches.' If sea and rocks proved too maddeningly difficult we fell back on a drawing of Carn Brea, a kind of local Fuji-Yama or holy hill. Tony paid us the compliment of severe criticism. To one of my attempts she said, 'Heather, dear? Oh . . . I thought it was an impression of the field of Waterloo after the battle.'

Perhaps it was the tea at the end that was the best part of the day. Like mother, Tony firmly believed in a spread on our return. There were splits and butter, apple cake, saffron cake, and lashings of cream. By the way, both in Cornwall and London jam was practically unknown to us, and what we saw of it in other houses we didn't like. Alice's 'jam every other day' carried no fun for me. Now if it had been 'apple cake every other day' I should have understood. This was made by filling a plate with pared apples, covering it with a round of pastry, baking it, reversing the crust, sugaring the apple, and spreading it over the crust. When cold, cream is added if you've got it. There was a lifelong feud between two of my aunts, because on one occasion the apple cakes had been salted instead of sugared, and each one declared it was the other who had done it.

When the big expedition to the North Cliffs was not on the cards, there were plenty of other pursuits in the place itself. There were two or three ponds, and a pond has great possibilities. One of these was cunningly placed in the side garden among tall elms inhabited by cawing rooks. Reflections of sky and trees were beautiful, but there was a memory round it. When mother was a girl, a large garden-party was being held at Reskadinnick and the guests were having tea, playing croquet, and strolling about on the front lawn, while the boys and girls were helping to entertain them. The youngest child, a little chap of four named Nicholas, had been given a piece of cake and had wandered down by himself into the side garden to play. After a while one of the guests noticed the beauty of the pond among the trees and walked down towards it. To his horror he found little Nicholas in the pond, into which apparently he had fallen, and either choked by a mouthful of cake, or unheard in the general talk, he had been drowned beyond hope of resuscitation.

'But what did they all do?' I used to ask mother when she told me this story. I suppose methods of reviving were unknown, for nothing could she remember except the anguish and self-reproaches of her mother. How one weaves fancies round those who never grow up, and what a real immortality they have! I have thought my Uncle Nicholas would have been the best of all, and grieved for him out of all proportion.

Another pond was of considerable size, occupying the whole of the end of the mowey. Here we let ourselves go. The boys made a raft of two stout planks, and by means of broomsticks were able to navigate the whole pond. A high hedge separated it from the field beyond, but here and there was a foothold on the bank where one could land. Each of these landing-places had some far-flung name—the Cape, Straits Settlements, Yokohama, and so on. One day we enticed the cook up into the mowey 'for a sail'. She stepped cautiously on board (*le mot iuste*), and before she could retreat Charles pushed off, and after a passage of peril and protest landed her at Madras. She was glad to feel the shore, but before she knew where she was Charles had put to sea again, leaving poor Temperance marooned. We other mariners in the home port shouted with joy, little considering that the family dinner was at stake. After raising the welkin to no effect, Temperance determined to try for an overland passage, and finally tore and scratched her way through the hedge into the lane. She was too devoted to the 'young gentlemen' to tell the grown-ups, and accounted for her scratches and the lateness of dinner in a way that would have satisfied Scotland Yard.

Not all our adventures on the pond could be so easily hidden. Barnholt and Edgar were once in possession of the raft, when Edgar invited me to come on too. 'It's all nonsense,' said he, 'about its only holding two, and you are only a little girl—your weight won't count,' and he held out his hand. Now I liked Edgar and trusted him, so on I stepped. The boys used their poles very carefully, and for a couple of yards all was well. But soon it was clear that our feet were wet. Another yard, and we were ankle-deep. 'Women and children first,' shouted Barnholt, and as the whole thing slithered into the pond, Edgar gave me a mighty push towards the shore. It was more mud than water after the first foot or two, and we were all too filthy to do anything but go straight back to the house and be hearty, and awfully sorry and generally comforted with baths and clean clothes.

Of course Lucy came out strong on the pond. She could not wait for her turn on the raft one day, and searched the barn for some rival craft. She found a large wooden case, without a lid, that seemed the very thing. There were visible chinks between the planks, but she didn't stay to caulk them. In the poultry-yard she found a tin bowl for baling purposes, and with her broom-pole leapt aboard the *Arethusa*, proclaimed herself Nelson off Copenhagen, and fiercely made for the raft, splashing the water at it as much as she could with cries of 'Surrender'. The boys sprang to the sea-fight with whoops of energy, one of them pushing towards Lucy, and the other splashing her. All were soon drenched, but that only heightened the excitement. We others on the shore shouted encouragement to both sides. But Lucy had the odds against her. Baling had to be constant, and although she managed a few swiping blows at the boys with her pole, every time she lunged at them the old chest listed heavily, and let in more water than any baling could cope with. Sinking, but fighting still, she was at last obliged to strike her colours, but we all felt that hers was a moral victory.

Many a time when the boys were off on some excursion of their own, far afield, and Beatrice was absorbed in domestic or social duties, Mina and I were left to ourselves. We had trained the grown-ups not to worry if we were late coming home. Tony was apt, however, to get fidgety if we did not turn up at dusk. 'Oh, my dears,' she would say, 'I was getting so hurried. I was afraid one of you had gone "over cliff."' 'Hurried' in Cornwall means 'anxious'; hence the saying: 'There was once an old woman who died in a hurry.' A tale was current about two little boys who went to the cliffs, one fell over, and the other was too paralysed with fright to go home until nightfall. This incident would seize Tony's imagination if any of us was late.

Apart, then, from a decently early return, nothing was expected of us. The authorities could rely on us to look after our own food-supply. I suppose no better education could be given two children than this freedom of the farm and country-side, and some of the happiest days of my life were spent with Mina, wandering about as chance directed. The grounds were so large that we were continually discovering some copse or hidden path or plantation that even Mina had not observed before. As a London child my ignorance about trees, poultry, and animals was complete, and all their ways were astounding. Warm eggs, eggs in the act of being laid, warm, foaming milk, a newly-born calf able to walk at once, absurd little chicks . . ., and Mina explained everything to me. The mill was a never-failing show-piece: we saw how the water managed to turn the wheel; we liked the jolly clack-clack of the works, and to bury our arms in the grain as it poured out of a wooden shoot. Another star place to visit was the forge. The old blacksmith generally had something going on. Bible miracles paled for me beside the incredible way in which he twisted a piece of red-hot iron just as his whim directed.

It was in the lane by the smithy that Mina and I had our one and only quarrel. I have no recollection of what it was about, but I was more blindly furious than at any other time in my life. I stammered out, 'You are a carcass.' I had no idea what the word meant, but it seemed to satisfy me and certainly roused Mina. We agreed to fight it out, and asked the blacksmith to see fair play. Mina was a little older and heavier than I was, but I hadn't had four brothers for nothing, and knew some bits of the noble art. Mina was soon running indoors, calling heaven to witness her wounds. Tony appeared, looked at the 'bruises', declared them to be only dirt, and to Mina's intense chagrin washed them off. I was then rather sorry for her, apologized handsomely for my dreadful word, and all was well again.

One place was our special home from home, and when we determined on a long visit to it serious supplies had to be collected. We raided the pantry for splits, the dairy for 'apple-meat', and the kitchen garden for any fruit in season—straw-berries, raspberries, gooseberries. A bottle of skimmed milk, or cider from the cask, a mug, and a book to read—all were stuffed into a basket, and we set off for the drive. About half-way down we plunged through the trees, crossed a brook, and found our objective, a giant oak. Now this tree had some strategic advantages. The trunk sloped at a convenient angle, but had no branches low down. At great pains we had cut little foot-holds which we knew how to use, but which escaped general observation. In fact the tree itself was barely visible from the drive, and when we were up the leaves hid us completely. The branches had contrived to twist themselves into comfortable seats with backs, and places to hang our basket.

When all was arranged we brought out the book. Only one, because a great point was its being read aloud in turn. We chose from the library shelves any book of Tales for the Young, and took much pleasure in prophesying the events. We could rely on Providence to punish the naughty and bring to notice the heroism of the good, and generally grant an early death to both. Why was there a bull in a field? To gore the disobedient. Why did cholera break out? To kill the child who went down a forbidden street. The names told us much : Tom, Sam, or Jack were predestined to evil, while a Frank could do nothing but good. Henry was a bit uncertain: he might lead his little sister into that field with bravado, or he might attack the bull to save her life at the cost of his own. We had bettings of gooseberries on such points.

One of our stories ran something like this:

THE LAST SHOP

A little girl who had a very rich mamma behaved herself so well one day that her kind parent said, 'Rosy dear, we will go for a walk down the street where the shops are, and you shall buy whatever you like, because you have been so good.' Skipping for joy little Rosy began to think of all the things she had been longing for. But mamma made one condition—that Rosy *must* buy something out of each shop. That seemed very easy, and the walk began well. A doll's perambulator in the first shop, some expensive lollipops in the next, some tarts at the confectioners, a pair of crimson slippers, some fancy-coloured note-paper, a whole pineapple, and a real writing-desk with secret drawers in it. In each case the purchase was ordered to be 'sent', and Rosy soon became anxious to go home in order to be ready to receive them. But mamma's face grew solemn.

'Have you quite finished, my child?'

'Oh, yes, thank you, dear mamma, pray let us return home.'

'I fear, my child, that there is *one* shop that you have omitted.'

So saying, she led Rosy to the undertaker's, and had her measured for a coffin. In this kind way, my dear young readers, little Rosy was early led to realize that death was the necessary end to all her pleasures.

This was among the more cheerful of the tales, for death itself usually befell the leading characters. Indeed, the mortality among children was so great that Mina and I wondered how any of them remained alive to grow up.

'How to improve Birthdays' was the promising title of one story. We were disgusted to find that it was all about a certain Caroline, who thought a great deal about her ailing mamma, ran upstairs to fetch things, amused baby, gave her dinner to the poor, and was beloved by young and old. Her new idea for a birthday was to give away to her friends, especially the poorer ones, all the things she liked best. At the head of the tale was a picture of unselfish Caroline, dispensing her books and toys to the poor, and among these gifts I noted a perfectly good paint-box. You can guess the text that was printed under this picture. We showed it in disgust to Tony, whose only comment was a snort, and 'Caroline's left hand seems to know all about it.' I studied the picture again, but could see nothing peculiar about Caroline's left hand.

As for the strategic advantages of our tree, an incident will best show what I mean. A certain visitor had been invited to tea. It must not be supposed that having any one to tea was the casual affair of to-day. An invitation would run a week ahead, special 'company' cakes would be prepared, involving much beating of eggs and squeezing of lemons, the table would be laid early with the crown Derby cups and saucers, and almost immediately after dinner would come a dreaded ordeal of extra washing and hair-doing and getting into best clothes, followed by a sitting quiet in case we got dirty again.

Now the Miss Tyack who was expected was an elegant young lady, pretty, polite, well dressed, and devoid of a single endearing failing. 'An oyster without a pearl' was mother's description of her. She neither talked nor functioned in any way beyond a watery smile and gentle assent to everything. Her visit therefore meant some three hours' hard work.

Mina and I got together and shabbily decided that we would escape. No sooner was the midday meal over than we faded out separately, selected some sample buns and cakes from the dishes already loaded for tea, and repaired to our ark. An afternoon of fearful joy lay before us—fear that we should be caught and brought back, and joy at out-witting the authorities.

Settled in the tree we found to our dismay that neither of us had thought to bring a book, and we didn't dare to go back to fetch one. So we agreed to play at being Charles II and Richard Penderel at Boscobel, with Miss Tyack filling the role of Cromwell's soldiers. The oak was in full September leaf, but now and again Mina would say to me, 'Your Majesty must keep your head a wee bit lower,' to which I would reply, 'A king fears nothing, my worthy Penderel.' Stories of Cromwell's cruelty were related, until the dramatic moment arrived.

'Hark, your Majesty!' whispered Mina. 'They approach!'

Hardly daring to breathe lest a twig should snap and betray us, we heard the mincing steps of Miss Tyack, and caught a glimpse of the pink ribbon of her hat. She drew level, and then passed, and as her footsteps died safely away we came near falling out of the tree with triumphant laughter.

Yes, we might laugh, but we hadn't reckoned on an hour or two of imprisonment. To make our game more real Mina had gone down several times into the wood and returned with 'food captured at the point of the sword from villagers'. In this dramatic way all our stock of provisions had been eaten.

We began to think enviously of Miss Tyack, how she was eating and drinking her fill, and being pressed to a little more. I was all for going boldly along, and bursting in on the company with some hearty tale of adventure, delay, mischance, no idea of the time, and what not. Mina didn't object to such deceit, but was horrified at the idea of appearing before visitors in her everyday frock.

Nothing would shake her, so at last I said, 'Well, Penderel, ourself will come to the aid of our distress. Do you remain here and keep watch.' So saying I slipped down the tree and made my way across a field at the back, and a long round that led eventually to the kitchen garden. Here I picked a large cabbage-leaf, filled it with raspberries, gathered a few apples, and stuffed them into the pocket of my pinafore. With enormous difficulty I made my way back to the faithful Penderel, spilling only a few raspberries *en route*.

When this spoil had been disposed of, and time began to hang heavy, I broached the idea that the enemy had already retreated, while I was away. Mina stoutly maintained that she had never ceased to watch, and we had to set our teeth and wait.

After what seemed like a year or two the longed-for sound of mincing footsteps broke on our ears like the strains of 'The Campbells are Coming' to the survivors of Lucknow. Running home we were too tired and out of spirits to think up any good excuse, and when we were greeted with a chorus of 'Where *have* you been?' we merely looked pathetic, fell upon the remnants of tea, and endured in silence the description of Beatrice's noble struggle to keep the conversation going with Miss Tyack. She and another elder cousin, Emily, were gaining such glory from their unselfish behaviour that we began to feel that we had positively occasioned it by our modest retirement.

To give a tea-party was bad enough, but to go to one was worse. An inevitable return invitation from the Tyacks arrived in due course, with the usual week's notice, precluding all chance of evasion. Beatrice and Mina, who had been well brought up with consciences in working order, immediately put this down to a 'judgement'. But Emily and I were more worldly, and as Emily pointed out, why should Providence be so stupid as to drag in herself and Beatrice, who deserved the best? These views were expressed at a private meeting in the garden.

'We shall have to play the piano,' said Beatrice.

'We shall have to go over the family album,' said Emily.

'We shall have to look through the stereoscope,' said Mina, 'and keep on saying how marvellous it is.'

'And they put sultanas into their saffron cake,' said I.

'I tell you what,' cried Emily excitedly. 'Let's not go.'

We laughed derisively, but she was full of her idea. 'Let's all be ill.'

As it was in mid-holiday, and we were in the rudest health, we looked at her inquiringly.

'Well,' said she, 'we've got a whole week, and if we refuse to eat all that time, we shall be too ill to go.'

'But how shall we keep from eating?' said I.

After a pause Beatrice had an idea for curbing our appetites. 'I will give two prizes to those who eat least in the time. We can watch one another and make a note of all that is eaten.'

'Let's see the prizes!' we exclaimed, and followed Beatrice up to her room, where she selected from her most sacred drawer two hidden treasures. The first was to be a gilt cross some four inches long, and the second was a wooden disk, with tiny toys in compartments round its edge; fixed to the middle was a pointer which you spun round and took the toy indicated. This was called a teetotum, and promised to be a wealth of magic delight. What was a little starvation, when such a prize could be secured?

We began well, for having made good dinners we were able to face a meagre tea. Nibbling our own bread and butter slowly, we watched one another's every mouthful. After tea Emily, who had been appointed to keep score, pronounced us all level. When supper-time was a repetition of this, Tony began to take notice.

'Whatever possesses the children? Have they been eating deadly nightshade, or wrong mushrooms, or something?'

'They've been stuffing themselves in the garden,' said Uncle Bill, and the matter passed.

Next morning Beatrice remained in bed with a 'sick head-ache', and asked for a cup of tea and one slice of dry toast to be sent up to her. This was grossly unfair, for by this means she was sure to get the first prize. Never mind, thought I, she is welcome to that old gilt cross, and there is still a chance of winning the teetotum. A scanty breakfast was followed by a Pacific Ocean of time to dinner. Either by chance or craft Tony had contrived a specially appetizing dinner, and when she pressed me to some chicken with 'eat it for my sake', I flung all chance of the prize to the winds, and fell upon it. At a meeting of the competitors in the afternoon, Emily con-fessed to having eaten raspberries on the quiet, and as I of course was out of the running, the teetotum fell to Mina. We all had to go to the party, and enjoyed it heartily in the mere fun of finding all our forebodings more than fulfilled.

Sometimes I would go forth quite alone, on some little errand for Tony, who said that a stranger from 'London town' would be impressive and entertaining to the numerous cottagers whom she befriended. I think that it was myself that was the more impressed usually. For instance, I was sent off to one of those cottages that have no privacy at all. I entered straight from the road, through the open door, into the living-room, and shall never forget the scene. Mrs. Polglaze, a cripple, was perched on a high chair in one corner of the tiny space. Seated on a couple of benches opposite her were seven or eight little children, mumbling aloud together, and laboriously pointing their fingers along what I supposed must be books. So black were these with use that no one could possibly read them, and the children must have been chanting from memory. Making my way through to Mrs. Polglaze I delivered Tony's pasties and fruit and butter, and was uncom-fortable at her extreme gratitude. I returned to Tony full of questions.

'Yes, dear,' said she, "'tis a real school. Poor old Mrs. Polglaze gets a penny a week for each child she takes.'

'But does she live on that?' I asked.

'Well, not entirely,' replied Tony, pushing off to her work.

Another task she gave me was more formidable. One of our numberless family cousins was an old lady of strong Wesleyan convictions, who lived in a large house in the town. She had expressed a wish to see Cousin Mary's little girl. Consequently I was made tidy and despatched. Mina stood by and darkly suggested that Cousin Jane would be certain to try to convert me. But Tony encouraged me by saying that I need not stay more than ten minutes, and 'You can go in on these', she added, giving me a bunch of fine geranium-blooms.

All went as scheduled. I entered brightly with the flowers, answered all the questions as to dear mamma's health, how the boys were doing at school, how long my holidays were to last, and generally kept my end up so well that I clean forgot any danger from religion. I had my trump card to get out on— that they would be getting hurried at home if I were late for dinner—and rose from my chair with easy confidence. Alas! Cousin Jane rose too, spread herself majestically between me and the door, raised her hand, and said,

'I trust, my dear child, that you have decided for the Lord?'

Now I had gathered from the boys that any one who is mad or drunk or peculiar in any way must be humoured. So with all the glowing enthusiasm I could muster I replied,

'Oh, *yes*, Cousin Jane!'

Seeing her look of extreme pleasure, I sought to complete my stroke, and added, 'Ra*ther*!'

At this she was so astonished that she was literally struck dumb, fell back a pace, and allowed me to slip past her, through the door, and out to freedom.

For one period every year there was a surfeit of out-door work for all. At harvest-time the whole place far and wide became a tornado of doings. Tony was anchored to the kitchen, producing portable food for the men in the fields and for us children. There was a great brewing of 'herby beer', which I once tasted because Edgar said it was good. Jars of this horrible liquor and of cider were everywhere available. The boys were all in two places at once. Uncle Joe was riding about on his horse, telling every one that this glorious spell of fine weather must be made the most of, for it surely couldn't last. And how we did work! There were no cutting-machines in those days, let alone binders. When I pass a harvest-field to-day I think how dull it seems. Yet how thankful Uncle Joe was when he was able to hire a machine for lifting the corn on to the rick.

Even I, the youngest of the crew, was able to do my bit, and I became quite an expert at binding, but could never equal the rate of the boys, who raced one another along the rows. Dinner-time was jolly. Not minding the heat we sat under one of the newly built corn-cocks, and devoured our pasties and cider. Then to work again, with no thought of anything so effeminate as tea, until dusk, when we returned to supper, weary and dirty, and went to bed early so as to be ready for the next day's work.

One day of my childhood was completely lost, and a glorious sunny day at that. Very rarely, for it was an expensive treat, the whole family, grown-ups and children, would go off to some distance for a long day. Sometimes it would be Penzance and the Land's End, sometimes the Lizard, sometimes Falmouth. It was usual to hire two long wagonettes, lunch at an hotel, and be free of the trouble of a picnic. Now a particularly favourite spot for such an expedition was Prussia Cove, which was full of possibilities, and more homely than the show places. There were little fishing-vessels in which we could have a sail. Shells of a rare and beautiful kind were to be found on the beach. Bathing was safe in the deep pools, and there were endless bits that we could sketch. The inn had once been the head-quarters of a famous old smuggler called the King of Prussia, and they could show you the false walls behind which he used to stow his kegs of brandy.

Well, one day we all set out for this desired haven, plotting during the long drive the special schemes that each had in mind. A big spread was to be provided for midday in the inn, and our only duty was to get up an appetite.

Arrived, my one and only thought was the sea. I ran on to a rock and promptly fell headlong into a pool.

'Oh, that's all right, darling,' said Tony. 'Come into the inn and we'll pop you into bed while we spread your clothes round the kitchen fire. They won't take above ten minutes or so.'

I fell fast asleep, and never woke until they were all getting ready to go home. I could have borne the misery of disappointment better if they hadn't said that they thought the sleep would do me good. As if one went to Prussia Cove for one's good!

XII

Indoor Doings

CORNISH people are nearly amphibious. Their peculiar mist of fine rain surrounds you in such a way that an umbrella is useless. Both this mist and slight showers are hardly regarded. But a steady downpour will occasionally keep you in if there is no pressing need to go out. On a really wet day, therefore, we children had to amuse ourselves indoors.

Although Reskadinnick was intricate and rambling enough to satisfy any child, it had a nucleus or nerve-centre round which the whole life of the place seemed to revolve. It was called the 'front kitchen', but had nothing of a kitchen about it. It had been the main living-room of the original old farm-house, but now served no definite purpose at all. Like some large-hearted friend it had no absorbing worries of its own, and was always empty and free for anything you wanted. Nowhere else have I come across a large room set aside for no purpose, and yet used continually. The dining- and drawing-rooms were solemnly devoted to Sundays and visitors; but the 'front kitchen' was far more dignified than either, in its homely aura of quiet.

Along one side of this room ran a row of casement windows, provided by nature with a long window-seat. This formed a perfect hiding-place if you stretched your length and kept your head down, because a colossal table of snow-white wood, hard as iron, was placed close alongside the window. The only other furniture consisted of a high-backed settle, a chair or two, and a grandfather's clock in a recess. At one end was the fireplace, with a high mantelpiece, holding two shapeless china animals, probably cats, always staring, reminding mother of the Cornishman who said his wife was 'no better than a cloamen cat'. The floor was paved with flagstones, never sanded as the ordinary kitchen was, and uncumbered by rug or carpet.

Here were held all family councils of moment, indignation meetings, and breaking of sad news. Here came Uncle Bill after he had written an important letter, to read it aloud, not to all the grown-ups together, but to each one in turn, to receive their admiration and slight improvements in the wording.

For one half-hour every day Tony would come here to 'do the milk'. The bulk of the dairy produce was sold to the cottages scattered over the downs, and for this purpose a stolid widow, named Mrs. Veal, trundled round a two-wheeled barrow holding a big container with tap attached. Very slowly she laboured up hill and down dale, without ever speaking a word apparently. Nothing could ruffle her, and goodness knows we tried hard enough. On her return Tony would take a seat at the great white table and spread out her business paraphernalia, consisting of a slate, a little account-book with pencil attached, and a kind of missionary box. I often slipped into the window-seat to listen to the rare sound of Mrs. Veal's voice, and marvel at her feats of memory. The ritual never varied: Tony read from her book the first name, thus: 'Mrs. Bray,' and Mrs. Veal would say, "Aporth and paid for et,' laying down a halfpenny on the table. Tony put this into the box, made an entry on the slate, and went on to the next name —Mrs. Pendray. Then Mrs. Veal: "Aporth and dedn't pay for et.' Another entry and another name. No one ever seemed to have more than a 'aporth, but many 'Dedn't 'ave any'. Watching this I hardly wondered that Mrs. Veal never indulged in idle chat, while her memory was functioning.

Once a week the big table was used for folding and ironing the huge family wash. For this purpose the irons were put in the fire till red hot and then slipped into brightly polished steel boxes with wooden handles—click, click they went over the enormous sheets and tablecloths. One day when Barnholt was tiny he insisted on walking on the table all in the midst of the operations. 'Heave 'e down, Miss Tony,' suggested one of the servants. 'No heave 'e down,' cried Barnholt, and heaved down he was not.

Apart from these domestic ceremonies the table was always available for anything that required elbow-room, such as wetting, stretching, and pasting on to boards the large sheets of drawing-paper that mother, Beatrice, and Charles used for their water-colour sketches.

Such a room positively called for theatricals, and not content with mere charades we once attempted a real play, a full-blooded melodrama, whose only light relief was the unintended. Charles and Beatrice produced it, and we underlings just did as we were told. Mina was pretty and made a fine heroine, but refused to sing in public. The operatic air that was essential for the piece had to be sung by Beatrice behind a screen, while Mina kept opening and shutting her mouth. Beatrice was the queen mother, Charles the heartless villain, and Edgar the hero. He had to look brave and say almost nothing. In fact he had but one speech: 'Draw your sword at once, Sir, and do not chatter.' This came at the crisis before the duel, but Edgar, who was quite word-perfect in it, and was tired of being the strong, silent man, always burst out with it before the time.

Rehearsals went on all day, and whenever the rain stopped we would run out and go over separate bits 'obscenely and courageously' in the garden. Old wardrobes and chests were ransacked for our dressings-up, and there was much competition for a blue quilted petticoat, a many-coloured silk shawl that mother had brought from Spain, and a black velvet cape lined with crimson. I say rehearsals, because the play never reached fruition. Not only did Charles and Beatrice come to continual loggerheads over the details, but the weather improved on us to such an extent that outside distractions were too strong for the team to be kept together.

However, as the dressing-up was the chief attraction, this we could do at any time for less ambitious acting. Getting away from the boys one afternoon, we plotted to take them in. Beatrice and Mina laid themselves out to dress me up as a nun. My forehead, ears, and throat were swathed in a towel (how hot I was!), a black kerchief was drooped over my head,

and a big black cloak pinned all round me. Then, watching
my opportunity, I staggered out among the trees a little way
down the drive, and thence approached the front door and
knocked. This door was not often used except by strangers,
and I had to wait till the housemaid had arranged herself to
answer it. I had prepared a humble voice, and begged to
see the lady of the house for a minute. I was then ushered
obsequiously into the drawing-room. Choosing a seat with
my back to the light I awaited my rather severe Aunt Knight.
Thankful that it was not Tony, who would have spotted me,
I began a most urgent appeal for a Home for Incurables.
Now this was the kind of thing Aunt Knight liked, and she
became quite emotional and full of inquiries. I worked myself
up in describing a bad case, and she left the room to fetch
a donation. At the door I heard her say, 'Do go in and speak
to her a moment, Tom, it all seems very sad,' and who should
come in but my brother, all politeness. I now pitched my tale
a little higher, describing the harrowing scene when a patient
was told that he was incurable, and should not we, who
enjoyed such robust health, &c. I had not expected to en-
counter my eldest brother, who was only on a short visit and
reckoned almost a grown-up, so what was my delight when
I saw him putting his hand in his pocket as he murmured
sympathetic dear-me's. When once I had grabbed his half-
crown, I unveiled, and when Aunt Knight returned with her
contribution she found us both in unseemly laughter.

Another time we all combined to disguise Charles as a
distant cousin, a lady from the Cape, impersonating some one
actually possible with a name that would 'go down'. Beatrice
provided a dress and a flowing hat, and a pair of glasses made
the get-up complete. When 'Miss Symons' had been ushered
into the drawing-room, my aunts hurriedly improved their
toilet, ordered tea to be laid in the dining-room, and swept in
all graciousness of welcome. Mother never bothered to alter
her attire for any one, but was equally taken in. Charles poured
forth an endless flow of patter about the flora and fauna of
South Africa, the beauties and dangers of the voyage, the

impertinence of his steward, and so on, answering all inquiries with careful accuracy (for we had prepared a few to ask him). All went swimmingly, and we were well through tea when Barnholt began to splutter, and the game was up.

It was an uncertain afternoon, neither rain nor shine, when some one started the idea of a war between boys and girls. It went with a swing. We girls agreed to remain in our big long bedroom, with windows on two sides, and pretend to be besieged in Lucknow. The boys were to be natives and make the attack. We sat tight and handed round apples as our last rations. Soon there was a thundering on the bolted door. At this we laughed, for it was only to frighten us. Next thing we knew was Edgar's head upside down at one of the windows. He knew the roof well and was hanging over. While we were making it hot for him with hair-brushes, Charles and Barnholt were at another window actually squeezing in. Our poor aims with pieces of soap and nail-brushes had no effect, and soon the battle was raging fiercely through the streets of Lucknow, round and under the beds, with pillows, bolsters, and knotted towels as weapons. When the place was a shambles, and sahibs and natives lying dead from laughter or exhaustion, Tony appeared to say what was all the noise and tea was ready.

Many a wet day was spent by Mina and me in exploring the house itself, in its cupboards, passages, and dark corners. In my grandfather's alterations and addition of the new house, the actual blending must have presented difficulties, and in one place a large empty space had been walled in between the new and the old. This space was the occasion for superstition. It was inhabited by a ghost, and possibly a skeleton. In Cornwall *omne ignotum pro mystico*. One of the 'new' bedrooms had a deep closet-cupboard standing immediately over this space, and the breakfast-parlour in the ancient part of the house had a cavernous cellar-cupboard running along underneath this space.

In one of our explorations of the bedroom closet, Mina and I heard voices in the cupboard below, obviously coming easily through the empty space. This suggested a chance of getting a thrill, and we looked about for some one to frighten. A housemaid at the time, named Eliza, was even more superstitious than most Cornish people. She believed it was the piskies who caused the milk to burn when put on the fire to scald, who induced the turkeys to lay astray, who snatched away Tony's keys when they were lost and found in her apron-pocket after a widespread hunt (a common occurrence). She was the very one for our victim. We waited for the day when she had to turn out that bedroom. Mina stationed herself on the main staircase, whence she could flit casually about. As soon as Eliza had swept the room and was about to sweep the cupboard, Mina fled downstairs to give me the signal. I went into the cellar-cupboard, and, in the most sepulchral tones I could muster, said,

'Eliza! Eliza!'

The movement of the broom, just audible to me, ceased. I then repeated my invocation, adding, 'All is known. Be sure your sin will find you out.' At this I heard a scream, and Eliza rushing downstairs. Making straight for Tony, she said nothing of what she had heard, but confessed with shaking sobs that she had stolen two of Miss Beetrice's handkerchiefs, and had eaten some of the apple cake in the dairy that very morning. Tony had to comfort her instead of scolding, and advised her not to go so much to those experience-meetings at her Wesleyan Chapel. Mina and I stood in the offing in quiet sympathy.

Among the treasures we rooted out from old wardrobes was an illustrated Prayer Book, gone quite brown with age and damp. When tired of reading we could get laughter out of its absurd pictures of fat angels and cupids on clouds, saints in imminent peril but elegantly arranged clothes, Isaac gaily stepping to be cut up, John the Baptist's head dripping on a dish, the Innocents being hurled about, and (a great find) a service for Charles the Martyr and another for the Gun-powder Plot, each with a picture of the critical scene. Foxe's *Book of Martyrs* was another feast for us, especially the picture of St. Lawrence on his gridiron. It was always this picture that came to my mind when I saw 'Trespassers will be Prosecuted' posted up, for it was many years before I distinguished prosecution from persecution.

We also found a Bible with the Apocrypha, and were astonished at the readable stories it contained. Susannah seemed to us a pretty and amusing tale, but it must be remembered that we were ardent readers of the *Arabian Nights*, without having the faintest idea of the cruder meanings of the episodes.

Not even the wettest day could keep us confined to the house itself for long. We would make a dash across the yards and over the lane to the barn, and sit reading there with a lapful of apples. Once we found the barn a foot deep in grain, and immediately began to swim in it, pretending to be Midas swimming in gold. Unfortunately we spoke of our swimming feats at the dinner-table and were forbidden in horrified tones to do it again. It seemed that it was not good for the wheat.

A still pleasanter city of refuge was the granary, a large loft stretching over the whole length of the stables. Its main attraction was the spice of danger in reaching it, as well as the feeling of security from detection when we were up. The ladder to it from the stables was not always in place, and when we had fixed it up it was always shaky. After mounting this ladder we had a nasty scramble through the trap-door at the top. Once up we could race to and fro to our hearts' content, and watch all the comings and goings in the yard, feeling superior to every one, even that horrible turkey-cock.

The boys were fond of rummaging in the Office. Here were a high desk and a chest, both containing documents, letters, plans of mines, maps, and account-books. They once unearthed some black stamps, many of which were valuable, being some of the earliest penny stamps ever issued.

When all else failed we fell back on drawing and painting in the front kitchen. I can remember no dull hour at Reskadinnick. And however dreadful the mess we made, Tony would always say: 'Where there is no ox the stall is clean.' As a child I thought this a funny remark, but now it seems quite otherwise.

XIII

A Family Club

LEAVING Cornwall was always a misery. Every accompaniment of it was miserable. We had to get up in the dark, choke down some breakfast, say good-bye to the cats, hope the station fly wouldn't come, wait on the lonely station platform for the fatal appearance of the train, scramble into any carriage, and worst of all wrench ourselves from Tony. Sometimes she would go as far as Truro with us, but that made the parting more prolonged and definitely worse.

However, spirits soon rose, for compensations became more weighty as the journey went on. Chief among these was the looking forward to seeing my father again, who was never able to spare more than a few days for a Cornish visit. We had heaps to tell him, and liked to show off our Cornish accent and turns of speech. For some time after our return we would say, 'Where's he to?' instead of the English, 'Where is he?' and 'Going out are you?' instead of 'Are you going out?' Tom had a theory that this method of putting the important word first came from our having been descended from the Romans. Our family name of Vivian was certainly of Roman origin. Some energetic member had the matter traced by experts, who 'discovered' to our immense delight that we were descended from the Roman centurion who jumped into the water crying, 'Desilite, milites!' To our fancy this brave invader fell in love with a Cornish maiden, and our lively family was the result, revelling in the motto: 'Dum vivimus vivamus'.

The name Vivian came in useful on our return journey, for our luggage was all labelled with it. At Paddington in those days all bags and trunks were arranged on the arrival platform under the letters of the alphabet. To find your belongings all you had to do was to go to the right initial. Since few people's names began with 'V', our baggage was to be seen in lonely state. It seems to me a good plan, for friends could also meet you at the initial. There we would find my father with cab engaged and all ready for us.

None but an old Londoner can understand the curious attraction of the town. After the music of the words 'London only' at Reading, we gave ourselves up to the *nil admirari* spirit. The size and importance of the terminus might alarm a timid fellow passenger, but were nothing to us. The wet streets (for it invariably seemed to rain on our return), the reflections from the street-lamps and the shops, the utter indifference of everybody to us and our concerns—why was it fascinating even to a child? I suppose we took on that feeling of superiority to all the world, the idea of finality, that London gives. No sign-posts to other towns are to be seen. Here's London. Here you are. We were almost of the same mind as the old Cornish farm-labourer who could not be made to believe that there was anything *beyond* London.

Mother's power of producing a spread on our return home was able to work at a distance, for my main recollection of coming into the house was a big meal laid ready on the dining-room table, and the excited talk of all our doings as we sat round it. My father and usually Tom as well had to be shown all our sketches, bits of Cornish stone and shells, and be told all our jokes and hairbreadth escapes. The grief at leaving Cornwall was definitely over.

A change came over our home life when Tom left Shrewsbury. His education, except for Latin and Greek, had to begin again, and he started preparing for a London degree. Dym taught him mathematics, for his ideas in that line were hardly better than mine. Although literature was almost part of the family furniture and not a 'subject' in those days, history had to be studied, for Shrewsbury had been aware of nothing later than the Roman Empire. French he read every day with mother.

With all this being done at home, and Dym preparing for a mathematics scholarship at Cambridge, the study became more a work-room than a play-room, and some kind of order had to be maintained. Now whatever else Tom had failed to learn at Shrewsbury he had acquired the knack of ruling others, and by common consent he became a kind of Dictator. A general meeting was held, and he divulged a grand scheme for organizing our life in the study on democratic lines. A family club was formed, to be called 'The Library'. The set of rules drawn up was to be as binding as the Decalogue. Like the Decalogue they were ten in number and chiefly negative. 'Thou shalt not' was the tone, but they did not interfere with the liberty of the decently behaved.

Although mother had nothing whatever to do with the affair, she must have been very glad of these rules, for they enabled the household to run smoothly without her having to harry, scold, or punish. Thus, in addition to regulations about work in the study, they forbade being late to breakfast (i.e. coming down after grace was said), going upstairs with boots on, omitting to brush your teeth, not hanging up coat and cap, and suchlike tiresome points for a mother to watch.

You may wonder how the club managed to enforce its rules. We all had definite pocket-money once a week, except me. I merely levied money from my father whenever I wanted some. Tom's plan was that we should be fined a penny, twopence, &c., up to sixpence, according to a definite scale of charges every time we broke a rule. He bought an account-book, assigned a page to each of us, and reckoned up how much each owed at the end of the week.

Still you may wonder how the payment of the fines was enforced. It was quite simple—no payment, no entry to the study. Since the study was the heart of our home, to be shut out of it was misery. Only once was there a failure to pay up. Barnholt was not recalcitrant, but bankrupt. I shall never forget the two days that he was shut out, wandering disconsolately about the house, doing his hateful lessons on the stairs. Mother was wrung with pity, and so indeed were all of us, but we dared not interfere with discipline by subsidizing him. However, I had private means, could stand it no longer, and

advanced him something . . . and Tom had the sense to make
no ugly inquiries.

Tom soon found what he had no doubt hoped—that we had
quite a nice little sum of money. He then unfolded his larger
plan: the club was to be a real library. The shelves that had
been decorated with childish fancies were cleared and made
ready for books, and the first outlay was to be an additional
bookcase that Charles had seen in Upper Street second hand.
The books themselves made quite a respectable show. Tom
had brought a good many from Shrewsbury, one of which
was actually a prize. Dym had plenty of prizes and a lot of
mathematical books. One I took to be *Comic Sections* was very
disappointing when I opened it. Charles and even Barnholt
had gained a prize or two, and we all had several gift books.
When we had levied some Scott and Dickens from the bookcase downstairs our shelves began to look businesslike.

Imagine our excitement when we found that soon after the
bookcase had been bought we had enough money to buy a
new book. The number of books suggested, the meetings we
held, the time spent in discussing the various possibilities—
it all seems beyond belief to-day, when books are so cheap. The
die was cast at last. Our love of *Ungava* determined us to get
another of Ballantyne's, and Tom was commissioned to buy
The Iron Horse. I asked Charles what it would be about. 'It'll
be something like the story of the wooden horse at Troy, I
hope,' said he. Surely no book was ever read and re-read and
talked over as that first new volume, although we went on to
buy many more.

One book we kept merely as a joke against Tom, for no one
ever opened it, and its pages were uncut. Tom had been sent
by my father to buy Barnes on St. Matthew. The bookseller
said he was sorry that he had not Barnes on St. Matthew, he
had only Barnes on Isaiah. 'Oh, that will do,' said Tom
amiably, and he bought it and took it home, to cause more
merriment than Barnes would have thought possible.

The outcome of our Library idea was an increased pride in
the room itself. We took it in turn week by week to dust and

tidy the study before breakfast. Since Tom didn't go to school
he had time after breakfast to make a tour of inspection, and if
he found any part undusted, or a book lying about, he charged
the weekly cleaner any fine he thought right, 'not exceeding
sixpence'. We never disputed his authority, for he took his
own turn quite fairly and paid up his own fines. However, he
had the privilege of being allowed to pay one of us to do his
cleaning.

For small misdemeanours, such as doing sums aloud, shaking the table, or spilling the ink, Tom executed summary justice
by means of a big, round, black ruler, that always lay on the
table like the mace in Parliament. 'Hold out your hand,' he
would say very quietly, and down would come the blow,
fairly softly if you were quick in holding out your hand. I was
spared the ruler, whatever I did, but otherwise was a full
member of the club for all privileges and penalties. And I was
an ever-ready runner of messages and fetcher of 'my india-
rubber, darling, on the hall table'. In fact stairs were my
hobby, for I could do three at a time. One day I was foolish
enough to defy Tom. He was busy, and told me to pick up a
piece of paper that had floated on to the floor. 'No, I won't,'
said I, rushing to the door. I saw Tom get up, and dreading
what he might do to me I fled in real terror to my bedroom,
and crouched down on the farther side of the bed and hid
under the valance. Tom followed at a leisurely pace, came
over, picked me up in his arms without a word, and carried me
up to the study. There he made my hand grasp the bit of
paper and place it on the table. I felt very foolish, and, strange
as it may seem, that is the only difference I have ever had with
Tom throughout our lives.

After a while we were in sufficient funds to take in some
magazines. *Sunshine* and *Little Folks* for the younger ones, and
Cassell's Family Magazine for us all. I can still remember the
deep interest I took in a long serial story called 'March Winds
and April Showers bring forth May Flowers'. To my great
satisfaction it didn't turn out to be all about nature, but
about a large family of boys and girls, who got into scrapes,

quarrelled, and made it up again, and had various jolly adventures. One short story in my magazine was amusing enough for the boys to read. 'Don't let the Joneses know' described some children going to a party. They were in distress because they had only a donkey-cart to go in. The rich Joneses were their special dread. These rich people would roll up in their carriage and pair, and would laugh if they heard about the donkey. 'Whatever you do, don't let the Joneses know'—that was the order of the day. Scheming by various delays to arrive late so as to slip in unobserved, they drew up at the precise moment that the Joneses had hit upon. Steeling themselves for the worst, they were astonished to find all the Joneses crowding round their cart, not with jeers, but with delighted admiration. 'How lovely! Look! A real donkey! And Harry driving it himself!' By this time the other guests had run out to look, and all were exclaiming, 'Oh, how we wish we had a donkey!' In fact they and their donkey were the main topic of talk and source of envy all the evening.

Mother specially liked this story, for it illustrated her oft-repeated injunction that for comfort and success in life one must never suppose that any other people whatsoever are one's social superiors, 'because,' she added succinctly, 'they aren't'.

Cassell's Magazine provided stronger meat, far more substantial than we get in the average magazine to-day. It had to last us a month, and I think every word of it found some reader in the family. When we had all read the portion of the serial story, and very definitely not before, we discussed endlessly at tea-time how the characters would turn out and who would marry whom. With so little new reading-matter to distract us we were able to carry all the details in our head until the next issue. The plot seems simple as I look back on it: a girl was engaged to a man whom duty bade her marry, while she was really in love with another. No one in those stories was ever actually married to the wrong man. To me the triangle seemed insoluble, and I was all prepared for a broken heart and tears. But Charles announced one day that the first young man would die, and all would be well. 'How do you know?' we asked him. 'I noticed him cough in the second chapter.'

Charles broke our rule of never discussing a book's plot with one still reading it, when he saw me one day deep in *A Journey to the Interior of the Earth*. 'Have you come to where they all die?' said he. I read on, expecting the worst on every page, until the end showed them all alive and well. I went to Charles in no little heat. 'Well,' said he, 'I never said they all died, I only asked you if you had come to it. And if you weren't a little silly you would know that they couldn't have *all* died, or who was left to tell the story?'

Wedding-bells were the usual end to our stories, of which *The Heir of Redclyffe* was a fair sample. Needless to say I had no notion of any difficulties after the bells had pealed. I took it for granted that husbands and wives were as happy as my own parents, with the exception of Aunt Bessie who grumbled at nothing, and Aunt Lizzie's husband who got drunk and threw things at her, a surely unusual case. *Vanity Fair* I read without the faintest suspicion of the intent of the note in the bouquet, or of Rawdon's reason for knocking down Lord Steyne. I thoroughly enjoyed that scene, although it seemed quite uncalled for.

One winter evening I was sitting over the fire engrossed in *Jane Eyre*, and had just got to where Grace Poole seems to be more than meets the eye, when Charles appealed to mother to take the book from me as being not very proper. She looked up, surprised, and then said, 'Oh, ah, yes, perhaps she had better not read it,' and took the book from me as suggested. Charles only meant it in fun, and was sorry that mother had taken it seriously, but the deed was done.

As a make-weight to our lighter magazines we took in the *Nineteenth Century*, and the elder boys read some of the articles. I struggled through one by Gladstone, in order to be able to say I had, but honestly I understood no single sentence. We were brought up in the belief that Gladstone was semi-divine, and to read an article by him ranked with reading the Bible.

However, Tom introduced a wholesome note of doubt on this point, and also on the absolute worshipfulness of Queen Victoria.

'I think she has had a pretty easy time of it,' said he, startling the tea-table, after one of mother's tributes to our beloved Queen.

'Oh, no!' cried mother, 'she has walked on the edge of a sword.' Thereafter I always pictured the Queen engaged in this absurd feat. I had been taken to see her once as she drove along Essex Road, and my memory of her made the idea of her walking on a sword merely funny. She was a shadowy figure to most people, but every one loved the Prince of Wales. He took a hansom once, and next thing you knew he might be in an omnibus. I asked mother what she would do if the Prince were to drop in to see us. 'I should offer him a little whisky and water,' was her immediate reply.

In the matter of religion as well as politics Tom knocked down a few family idols. My father was a dark horse in these directions, but now and again let loose a delightfully irreverent remark. A Wesleyan concert was billed 'to commence at 7.30 D.V.' 'Good Lord!' cried my father. 'Do they suppose the Almighty is going to bother about the time of their blooming concert?' But as a rule he let mother's piety have full sway. And it really did little harm, for it was concerned with externals almost entirely. Thus we were not allowed to put any other book on the top of the Bible. We knew the dreadful story of the little girl who couldn't reach a shelf, trod on the big family Bible to help her, fell, and of course died of her injuries. So you can imagine the shock I got when Tom spoke lightly to mother about Elijah's sacrifice on Carmel.

'Petroleum was what he poured on the altar. He had a secret store of it, as all those holy men had—Moses on Sinai, and every time there was "fire from heaven".'

When mother expostulated, Tom said, 'Well, then, where did Elijah get all that water when there was not a drop to be had?'

Mother was still unconvinced until Tom told her of a passage in Maccabees, which explained the whole thing, and said where the petroleum was stored. He said that Elijah had no idea of humbugging the people, but thought God had given him this 'holy water' to use for His glory. At this mother was quite excited at the new light on an old difficulty. Still she was not clear how the petroleum caught fire. Tom looked round, saw me in the corner, and told me to run upstairs to the study and fetch Dym's magnifying glass.

'Now, mother, come out into the sun,' said Tom, 'and I'll soon show you.' In a few moments a piece of thin paper was scorched and actually alight.

'But Elijah hadn't a magnifying glass,' said mother.

'Oh, yes, he had. Those prophets knew lots of scientific facts, but kept them as holy secrets, entrusted to them by God, to be made use of for His glory. Look at their weather forecasts, their cure of diseases, their poison-antidotes. A magnet was a miracle.'

I was rather alarmed at all this, and was surprised to see how unhorrified and really interested mother was. I half expected to see Tom himself struck dead by an outraged Jehovah.

In the summer of 1877 Tom started a new idea. Not content with our magazines, he suggested that we should make one of our own. Of course we took up the idea with fervour, and meetings were held to decide the paper to be used, the size of the page, the material and colour of the cover. Its name was *The Bee*, because it was to go from flower to flower collecting honey for its readers, as Tom explained in a poem on the first page. He, of course, was the Editor, Dym the science special correspondent, Charles 'our artist' and provider of light fiction. But there was very little light about the publication, in which everything was expressed as solemnly as possible.

We had no reproducing machine, so that it all had to be written in manuscript. In order to preserve uniformity of appearance Tom copied it all himself. He sat at one end of the study table, and it was a point of honour not to look. Charles did a water-colour frontispiece for each number, one of Canonbury Tower, another of St. Paul's from Merchant

Taylors' School playground, and a large number of pen-and-ink illustrations. I was allowed to do some little tail-pieces.

Tom wrote heavy articles in the style of the *Nineteenth Century*, on such subjects as 'The effect on Poetry of Science', 'The Penge Case', and 'The Ritualists'. Charles described Wagner's *Lohengrin*, and provided a serial story. Dym wrote on Voltaic Electricity, with diagrams of test-tubes and things, and on the Russo-Turkish Relations. I managed an account of a picnic in Cornwall, and a poem on my cat. I can remember pacing up and down my bedroom in torture of composition for my last line, which was rung out at last with more truth than rhythm. The final stanza ran thus:

> *Of a very bad cough*
> *Poor Pinky died,*
> *But I must now finish off,*
> *Which to do I've often tried.*

Tom kept to himself that in the original her fatal disease was spelt 'coff'.

Tom got blood out of a stone, for he actually extracted a contribution from Barnholt. There was a symposium in the November issue on 'Flogging at School', on which each expressed his opinion. Barnholt produced no fewer than twenty-two lines on the subject. His opening remark was arresting: 'Flogging is a very good substitute for boys who will not work.' The burden of his article was that any punishment was better than endless detentions.

Each number of *The Bee* was placed by my father's side at the breakfast-table, that he might have the virgin glance. His genuine admiration and pride were ample reward for all our trouble. It was then passed round the family to be read in turn, and such care did we take of the five numbers we produced that they are still as clean to-day as when they left Tom's hands, and the fifty years and more have hardly faded the ink. I am still fond of poring over them, all except Barnholt's little essay, which I find too much of a human document . . . so many hours of his short life to have been spent in senseless detention!

XIV

A Last Christmas

THE jolliest winter of our childhood was in 1878. We had only given up making our magazine because real work was too pressing. Tom was at the last phase for his B.A. and Dym was in full hopes of his Cambridge scholarship. Charles had left school in order to give his whole time to his water-colour painting. Most of his days were spent in town, copying the technique of David Cox, Turner, and Muller, and we all looked forward to seeing what he brought home every evening. He had sold so many of his own original sketches that he confidently hoped to make his living in that way.

Of the four boys Barnholt was perhaps the happiest. Released at last from his eternal 'detentions', he had been taken from school and placed in a shipping office, with the prospect of next year fulfilling the dream of his life by going to sea. As mother had predicted, he was the first of us to earn his living, to have a real salary, to be a 'man of means'. I fancy that he had suffered a good deal from having to wear the other boys' left-offs, for the first thing he did was to buy quite quietly a new suit. I can see him now as he walked into breakfast in it. It was a grey tweed, bristling with newness, and we were all full of admiration as he went off with my father 'to the City', while mother proudly demanded to know what she had told us.

And I too was happy in the first flush of my school-days, involving important 'homework' at the study table. At my October birthday the family came out strong: Tom bought a papier-mâché pencil-box that shut firmly and had Chinese figures doing something on the lid. Inside were three compartments. In the longest of these Charles put five new lead pencils (ranging from HH to BB). In the middle-sized division

Dym put a penknife, and in the smallest division Barnholt put a piece of soft india-rubber. Mother gave me a pair of scissors to be entirely my own, and my father brought me home the loveliest umbrella ever designed. It was of dark blue silk, and had a carved ivory handle. He must have given a lot for it, and I could never bring myself to use it. I carried it to school every day firmly grasped round the middle, but never opened it. When I was driven, one day much later, by a sudden shower to loosen the elastic band and spring it open, what was my dismay to find the silk in shreds where my hand had worn it.

The pencil-box was the envy of my school-fellows. The boys were greatly tickled at the way in which I assigned a special pencil for use in the various subjects—a history pencil, a geography pencil, and so on. 'I say, Molly, lend us your Scripture pencil,' Dym would say, for he knew that was an H, and good for his geometry figures. They all took an amused interest in my lessons and my 'little friends', as they called my school-fellows. My father, too, used to ask what I was doing, and one day, by way of reply, I inflicted on him the recitation of a whole poem about Mary Queen of Scots. This began:

I looked far back into other years, and lo, in bright array.

I haven't the faintest notion now of what I saw in bright array, but the closing lines have stuck in my memory. They refer to the blood of the queen, and run thus:

The noblest of the Stuart race, the fairest Earth hath seen,
Lapped by a dog! Go, think of it, in silence and alone,
Then weigh against a grain of sand the glories of a throne.

Neither I nor my father thought of carrying out these instructions, but he gave me sixpence and said it was very good.

He used to help me with my sums, going very slowly with his explanations and telling me about things they did 'in the City'. He taught me how to write quickly by never taking off my pen in the middle of a word, and gave me 'transubstantiation' to practise on. I aimed at copying his handwriting, which I still think the best I have ever seen. When he noted my ambition he said, 'Yes, all right, only be sure you never copy my, or any one's, signature—never on any account, even in fun.' So he could be quite serious at times, but as a rule he couldn't resist taking me in, because I was such easy game. 'I saw a nigger in the City to-day who was so black that charcoal made a white mark on him.' How that worried me! But I took in as Gospel the story of the man who bought a bottle of hair-restorer, dropped it on the door-step while he was fumbling for his key, and spilt it all—only to find next morning a fine hair mat outside.

My ideas about the City were confused. Sunday showed me a peaceful wilderness, where one walked in the middle of the road. Barnholt's accounts were of crowds of people, and the following scrap of conversation between father and mother didn't help matters.

'Seen any one in the City to-day, Tom dear?'

'Not a soul, except old Herring.'

I pictured a herring suspended somewhere on a string across the street. Mother didn't seem in the least surprised at the lack of population.

To us one November evening there came a casual knock at the door, and who should walk in but Tony. Better than the comfort of being met at the station was the joy to her of giving us all such a surprise. As we crowded round her she explained that she had just 'slipped away' to spend a week or two with us. A telegram would seem to have been the natural thing to send, but in those days telegrams were nearly always reserved for disasters, so that the yellow envelope in itself was a shock, and care was taken that the person to whom it was delivered should be seated ready for the worst. Tony laughingly said she was sure of a welcome, and knew that mother could always throw up a bed.

She then disclosed that she had not come alone, but was to be shortly followed by a barrel of apples and a young pig, coming on by goods train. The barrel was delivered first and was installed in the china-closet near the front door, and we had full permission to help ourselves whenever we liked. The

young pig, technically known as a 'porker', arrived wrapped
in canvas on the carrier's shoulder, and was laid on the kitchen
table ready for cutting up. It seemed to involve the whole
household in feverish activity for days. There was glory for
the servants, since all regular work was pushed aside in the
effort to find big earthenware pans, to fetch in saltpetre and
treacle, and clean up. The boys were summoned to help cut
the big joints, and to pack up some of them to be sent to relations. I helped chop up the small meat ready for mother and
Tony to make into sausages and pork pies.

Naturally Tony wanted to see the shops, and as soon as the
Christmas holidays began I was allowed to go with her and
mother to the West End. Tony was all for taking hansoms.
As she pointed out, a bus can be taken any day—a holiday was
a holiday, and she didn't believe in doing things by halves.
She argued that it is the regular expenses that one should
worry about, not the occasional. So she took hansoms right
and left, and I can still recall the luxurious feeling of snuggling
down in a hansom between her and mother, to be wafted
exactly where we wanted to go. I could just see the toss of
the horse's head and could hear the klip-klop of his hoofs
and the cheerful jingle of his bells. It is amusing to reflect now
that the bells on a hansom were put there as a warning to
pedestrians to get out of the way of such swift vehicles. Those
were the days when a man with a red flag used to walk in front
of a steam-roller. I wonder what Tony would say to the traffic
in Piccadilly to-day. On one of her later visits to London I took
her on the top of a bus, to see some of the life of the town. As
I called her attention to this and that, she said, 'Don't ask me
to look, dear. If I take my eye off the driver he will surely run
into something.'

What she suffered in a hansom I can't imagine, for she had
no control over the driving, even with her eye. But in 1878
the traffic was laughably simple, and the only likelihood of an
accident was the slipping of a horse on a wet road. Even then
the driver from his high seat could usually pull the horse to
his feet again. But mother would never let the glass window

in front be used, however hard it might rain, because a sudden fall of the horse might easily throw us headlong through the glass.

A morning's shopping was all we could manage for one day, for, strange as it seems now, the big shops had no restaurants, no rest-rooms, no conveniences for toilet, however dire one's need. The first tea-shop was opened at London Bridge, out of sheer pity for lady customers!

Much energy was spent in restraining Tony from buying too many presents, for the shops were so enticing. We found it safer to take her for expeditions to Epping, Hadley Woods, and Kew. One day I was allowed as a great treat to take her up to Hampstead Heath all by myself. Inducing her to tell me stories, I distracted her attention (and apparently my own) from the route we were following. At a strategic point I stopped suddenly, looked bewildered, and declared that I had lost the way. In reality I had led her in and out among short lanes and little paths, to and fro, and was all the time within easy distance of the station. At first I enjoyed seeing how 'hurried' she became, but when she talked of looking for a policeman, finding a post office, and telegraphing to mother, I thought it was time to discover the station, and with a bright 'Here it is after all!' ushered her into the booking-office.

As Christmas drew nearer we had several evening gatherings, not formal enough to call parties, for the boys and their friends. Charles called them 'Robin Adair' parties, because a girl we knew used to trill forth this song on the slightest pressure. Aunt Polly would always oblige with 'Tell them they need not come wooing to me', occasioning many ribald remarks from the boys. Another song that became familiar was 'She wore a wreath of roses'. No one knew why she had this head-gear, and when the poor fellow saw her again she had changed it. 'Methinks,' he sang, 'I see her now, with a wreath of orange-blossoms upon her marble brow.' One evening my father was begged to sing a song, and what was our astonishment when he stood out on the hearth-rug and without any accompani-ment gave forth 'The Bells of Aberdovey', in glorious rich tones. Seeing every one's pleasure no doubt heartened him on, and his careless unconcern enabled him to get the full effect of the lovely Welsh words.

One of Tony's presents was a magic lantern, which she delivered before Christmas, so that the boys might practise it beforehand. Wonders are so thick to-day that no child can understand my thrill at the darkened study and the sight of coloured figures chasing one another in mid-air.

Everything combined to make this Christmas (the last we were to have all together) the best of all. Ambitious now with their acting, the boys attempted a real play—*Box and Cox*. Tom and Dym took the title-roles, and Charles that of Mrs. Bouncer. Happily for me there was no heroine, and I could enjoy it all to the full. There was Dym cooking a chop over the study fire, and only leaving in the nick of time before Tom came in all hatted and overcoated, and there was Charles always in a dither. The whole thing was a success, loudly applauded by the grown-ups, including Tony and several others. A magic-lantern display followed, and then we all assembled downstairs for the presentation of Christmas gifts.

This was on a larger scale than ever before. The boys joined forces to give me *Aventures d'Alice au Pays des Merveilles*. They were proud of this book because the translation had been done by Henri Bué, the French master at Merchant Taylors'. My curiosity was to see how he had put into French 'Off with his head!' and I was amply satisfied with the funny way he rendered it.

Barnholt guessed rightly that I wanted a more frivolous note, so he added to my pile a mouse that would run along the floor when wound up. All other presents have slipped my memory, with the grand exception of those we children gave my father. We had each bought him a book, and my vividest memory of him is that jolly scene. There he sat, gazing at the pile of five books—too pleased to speak, too pleased to touch them.

The November of 1879 was cold and dark with fogs far worse than ever happen now. We used to look out to see torches being carried, and making ghastly glares in the deep yellow. One evening my father did not return. He had been run over and instantly killed. They did not dare to tell mother. She went next day into the City to inquire, and was told by my uncle that Tom had been called away on business to Don-caster. And she waited somehow till two days had passed, when they came and broke the news. During the years that followed she used to sit in the dusk, in a chair facing the gate, as she had waited for Barnholt years before. I think she almost hoped that the past was only a nightmare, and that she would surely see my father coming up the garden path with his springy step, and would hear his familiar knock.

Oxford Paperbacks

OTHER BOOKS BY M. V. HUGHES

A LONDON GIRL OF THE 1880s

In this sequel to *A London Child of the 1870s*, equally charming and delightful, Molly Hughes continues her account of growing up in Victorian London. All the hardships and triumphs of school life, the pleasure of outings to museums and theatres, and the comforts of an affectionate family are remembered and recorded in vivid detail.

A LONDON HOME IN THE 1890s

The final book in Molly Hughes's autobiographical trilogy covers a decade crammed with adventure: a new career in a teacher training college, travels to Europe and America, and marriage to Arthur Hughes in the year of Queen Victoria's Diamond Jubilee. The birth and tragic death of her daughter are movingly related, as is – more light-heartedly – the election campaign in which her husband stood against Lloyd George.

A LONDON FAMILY BETWEEN THE WARS

The Hughes family – a widow with three sons – were not well off financially, but were rich in affection. This is a gentle, often humorous account of a family growing up in the rural environs of London in the 1920s and 1930s. It recaptures the charms of a now vanished world, in which *The Times* arrives by bicycle, household necessities are supplied by a hawker with a pony cart, and making a telephone call is an adventure.

STILL GLIDES THE STREAM

FLORA THOMPSON

Like her well-loved trilogy *Lark Rise to Candleford*, this book depicts the vanished life of the countryside which Flora Thompson knew as a child in the 1880s. Cast in a fictional form, it is an enchanting portrait of an Oxfordshire village and its inhabitants around the time of Queen Victoria's Golden Jubilee.

'. . . reading it is a perfect pleasure' *Benny Green*

THE GAMEKEEPER AT HOME and THE AMATEUR POACHER

RICHARD JEFFERIES

With an introduction by Richard Fitter

First published in 1878 and 1879, these two books nostalgically recapture the sights, characters, and pastimes of the nineteenth-century English countryside.

THE JOURNALS OF DOROTHY WORDSWORTH

Edited by Mary Moorman

Wordsworth's 'exquisite sister', as Coleridge described her, was not only the cherished companion of two great poets, but was herself a poet in prose. The journals she kept at Alfoxden in 1798, when her brother and Coleridge were composing the *Lyrical Ballads*, and at Grasmere from 1800 to 1803, when she and Wordsworth were living at Dove Cottage, are more than a valuable record of their daily life. Dorothy combined an intense and minute observation with a genuine poetic imagination, whose influence can be seen in many of Wordsworth's poems of this period (printed at the end of this book).

GUIDE TO THE LAKES

WILLIAM WORDSWORTH

Complete with illustrations, notes, and a map, this is the best-selling guide to the part of England that inspired one of its greatest poets.

'. . . the archetypal book for the Lake District connoisseur . . . a classic of committed prose about a passionately loved landscape'
Melvyn Bragg

THE DIARY OF A COUNTRY PARSON

JAMES WOODFORDE

Edited by John Beresford

James Woodforde was an eighteenth-century Norfolk parson, a *bon vivant* with a passion for food and a healthy appetite for drink, sport, and gossip. Ever since its discovery early this century, his classic diary has entranced readers with its vivid portrait of daily life in the rural England of two centuries ago.

A VICTORIAN POACHER

JAMES HAWKER'S JOURNAL

Life was hard in the mid-eighteenth century, especially for the son of a village tailor, so James Hawker took to poaching. To the day of his death at the age of 84 he continued to outwit the exasperated, yet admiring gamekeepers of the Leicestershire estates he plundered. His diary reveals him to be a shrewd, vigorous, and humorous man, and speaks eloquently of country lore, wildlife, and the poacher's craft.

Oxford Paperbacks about Ireland

THE WESTERN ISLAND or THE GREAT BLASKET

ROBIN FLOWER

Covering the years 1910 to 1930, this is an illustrated account of the folklore and life of the Great Blasket Island, three miles out into the Atlantic to the west of County Kerry.

THE ISLANDMAN

TOMÁS Ó CROHAN

Tomás Ó Crohan was born on the Great Blasket Island in 1856 and died there in 1937, a great master of his native Irish. His account of the harsh life there is a valuable and fascinating record of a now vanished way of life.

AN OLD WOMAN'S REFLECTIONS

PEIG SAYERS

'The Queen of Gaelic story-tellers' passed the greater part of her long life on the Great Blasket Island. Here she reflects on the days of her youth spent on her beloved island.

THE ARAN ISLANDS

J. M. SYNGE

In this book, illustrated by his own photographs, the famous Irish playwright recounts his travels and encounters on the Aran Islands He describes the magic wells, poteen drinkers, and fishing expeditions in currachs, and records the stories told him by the solemn Pat Dirane of islanders who fell victim to the druids and the fairies.